In
Pursuit of
Freedom

WILLIAM C. KASHATUS

In Pursuit of Freedom

Teaching the Underground Railroad

FOREWORD BY **James Oliver Horton**
AND **Lois E. Horton**

HEINEMANN
Portsmouth, NH

Heinemann
A division of Reed Elsevier Inc.
361 Hanover Street
Portsmouth, NH 03801–3912
www.heinemann.com

Offices and agents throughout the world

The author and publisher wish to thank those who have generously given permission to reprint borrowed material:

Figure 1–1: "Map of the National Underground Railroad Routes, 1860." Reprinted by permission of the Chester County Historical Society, West Chester, Pennsylvania.

Figure 3–1: "Frederick Douglass, ca. 1848." From a daguerreotype by an unidentified photographer, ca. 1848. Reprinted by permission of the Chester County Historical Society, West Chester, Pennsylvania.

Figure 3–2: "Harriet Tubman, ca. 1845." Courtesy of the Library of Congress.

Credits continue on p. vi.

Library of Congress Cataloging-in-Publication Data
Kashatus, William C., 1959–
   In pursuit of freedom : teaching the Underground Railroad / William C. Kashatus.
      p.   cm.
   Includes bibliographical references.
   ISBN 0-325-00652-0 (alk. paper)
   1. Underground railroad—Study and teaching (Middle school).   2. Underground railroad—Study and teaching (Middle school)—Activity programs.   3. Fugitive slaves—United States—Study and teaching (Middle school).   4. Fugitive slaves—United States—Study and teaching (Middle school)—Activity programs.   I. Title.

E450.K269 2005
973.7'115—dc22   2004020396

Editor: Danny Miller
Production editor: Lynne Costa
Cover design: Night & Day Design
Typesetter: Kim Arney Mulcahy
Manufacturing: Steve Bernier

Printed in the United States of America on acid-free paper
09   08   07   06   05   VP   1   2   3   4   5

*For Barbara Jobe, Suzanne Halstead, and Stephen Watters,
master educators and supportive colleagues.*

Contents

Foreword

On July 5, 1852, a crowd of some six hundred people gathered in Rochester, New York, at Corinthian Hall to hear Frederick Douglass, the great voice of abolitionism, speak. Douglass began his lecture by asking why he had been called upon to speak and then posed a question that stunned the audience. "What to the slave is your Fourth of July?" he asked. With this question Douglass exposed America's central and most blatant contradiction. A nation founded on the principle of human freedom as an inalienable God-given right condoned and protected the system of human slavery upon which its economic system was founded.

Slave labor produced America's most important item of world trade. By 1840 slave-produced cotton was more valuable than everything else the nation exported to the world combined, making the value of human property enormous. By the time of the Civil War, barely eight years from the time of Douglass' lecture, the dollar value of slaves was greater than the dollar value of all American banks, railroads, and manufacturing combined. Bound human beings were in fact more valuable than anything else in the country except the land itself. With such economic significance, slavery and those who supported it held a disproportionate share of national political power.

Slaveholders occupied the American presidency for fifty of the seventy-two years between the election of George Washington and the election of Abraham Lincoln. By the time of Douglass' speech, slavery's supporters controlled the major committees of both houses of Congress and of the U.S. Supreme Court. Slavery was not a minor labor system of the American South. It was a major national institution that also enriched Northern merchants, international traders and financiers, and New England cotton textile manufacturers. It was as politically powerful as it was economically central to America's national and international relationships.

The economic and political power of slavery was enough to encourage some Americans to attempt to ignore its horrors, to overlook its un-American character. Slavery was a hypocrisy so immense that the founding fathers could deal with its existence only with relative silence and indirection. The word was not written into the Constitution and the institution was referred to only euphemistically in an effort to persuade South Carolina and Georgia, the nation's most slave-dependent states at the time, to accept the Constitution. Yet there were Americans, whites as well as blacks, who could not and would not ignore slavery's evil and its inhumanity. As formal organizations, as small ad hoc groups, or as single individuals whose personal morality could not tolerate human bondage, some Americans opposed the existence of slavery in a free America. The Underground Railroad, an informal network that aided fugitives from slavery in their search for freedom, was an important part of that opposition.

William C. Kashatus' *In Pursuit of Freedom* takes on the myth and the reality of the Underground Railroad with a balanced perspective that will help teachers provide students with a complex story both faithful to the historical record and respectful of oral tradition. He also provides a clearly and concisely written short history of slavery. Growing out of the Chester County Historical Society's *Just Over the Line* exhibit on the Underground Railroad, this book is based on a deep understanding of southeastern Pennsylvania's clandestine struggle for black freedom and extends that understanding to provide a general context for escapes from slavery in other areas of the country as well. Students in today's multiracial society can benefit from such in-depth study of the Underground Railroad and slavery because it defies easy generalizations, engages the students' moral sense, and promotes critical thought.

With a keen understanding of learning styles and the developmental stage of middle school students, Kashatus offers well-tested exercises in reading and interpreting documents, photographs, and engravings, as well as suggestions for active learning such as decoding songs and participating in plays and reenactments. Typical of the thoroughness of his work are the suggestions for role-playing exercises that go beyond the usual dramatization of escapes to include discussions about antislavery conventions and the everyday decisions of shopping for products produced by free labor.

Throughout, this work engages students and teachers in discussions of values and raises important issues that will both link students to the past and connect them to contemporary concerns. Teachers will find useful advice on helping students engage in original research in local history. Examples of different levels of student work with primary source materials will also provide guidance on creating and evaluating assignments. An annotated bibliography that includes books, videos, and websites will be valuable to students and teachers alike. The bibliography is aimed primarily at students in grades 4 through 8, although it contains some material appropriate for students up to grade 12.

In Pursuit of Freedom: Teaching the Underground Railroad provides teachers with a rare combination of historical context, analysis of important historical issues, and practical guidance. It offers an opportunity for teachers and students to consider the responsibilities of individual citizens in a democratic society.

James Oliver Horton and Lois E. Horton

Acknowledgments

In Pursuit of Freedom would not have come to fruition without the financial assistance of the Chester County Historical Society. Roland H. Woodward, CCHS president and director, and the board of trustees gave their unwavering support to the school partnerships upon which the material in this book is based as well as to the publication of this book.

Just as important was the active participation and commitment of the schools. Patricia Kelly and Dr. Beverly Trosley of Ridley Middle School and Terrence Maguire of Wilmington Friends School supervised their students' work and added immeasurably to the orientation, development, and logistics of the project. I am extremely grateful for their efforts and those of their students, whose work appears in these pages: Bob Andrews, Michelle Casey, Ashley Evans, Heather Hall, Danielle Hart, Caitlin Hitchens, Dana Kozubal, Ada Plesati, Victor Poiesz, Frank Taddie, Tara Tavernia, Christian Willman, and Ashley Yezuita of Ridley Middle School; and Kelsey Burston, Megan Garrett, Sean Mansory, Ali McKay, Drew Rizzo, Michaela Snead, Ayana Suber, and Emily Swain of Wilmington Friends School.

Several individuals deserve thanks for the preparation of the book. Dr. James Oliver Horton of George Washington University, and Dr. Lois E. Horton of George Mason University, both noted scholars on the Underground Railroad, kindly agreed to write a foreword; Mary Michals of the Illinois State Historical Library, Pamela Powell of Chester County Historical Society, and artist Dane Tilghman gave their permission to reprint illustrations for the book; and Danny Miller of Heinemann gave his remarkable editorial skill as well as his constant encouragement for the project.

A special debt of gratitude goes to my colleagues at CCHS, who were instrumental in transforming a personal dream to do a major exhibit and educational programming on the Underground Railroad into a reality that captured national attention. Ida McIntyre, our business manager, kept me on budget, while Deborah Lane, our shop manager, came up with a thousand ideas and products to promote the exhibit and the educational programming. Ellen Endslow, Rob Lukens, Pam Powell, Diane and Laurie Rofini, and Wes Sollenberger of the Collections Department offered constructive counsel and the sweat equity to make the exhibition work. Jessica Files and Anthony Stavenski, summer interns in the Education Department, contributed their enthusiasm, hard work, and creativity and allowed me to share some of their ideas in this book.

My colleagues in the Education Department—Barbara Jobe, Suzanne Halstead, Terry Schwabe, and Sarah Wesley—gave me their counsel and hard work during the last five years. Barbara and Suzanne, in particular, were always there for me, nurturing my understanding of the museum field, contributing innovative educational programming, listening to my frustrations, and offering a kind word when it was most needed—all while somehow tolerating my unusual sense of humor. Words cannot adequately describe my appreciation for their efforts; I can only honor them with the dedication of this book.

Just as important an influence was Stephen Watters, head of Green Vale School in Long Island, New York. During his years as head of the middle school at Philadelphia's William Penn Charter School, Stephen had a profound impact on my ideas about teaching preadolescents. His extensive knowledge of and passion for that age group as well as his guidance, personal example, and friendship have been among the greatest blessings in my teaching career. I will always be grateful to him for those gifts.

Finally, I am grateful to my family—my wife, Jackie, and our sons, Tim, Peter, and Ben. They have given me not only their unconditional love and support but also the peace of mind to face life's trials on my own terms and never regret it. My love for them is eternal.

Introduction

The Underground Railroad is a subject of endless fascination for teachers and students alike. Their interest has been inspired by the current national dialogue on race, which encourages black and white Americans to look to the past for incidents of racial cooperation.[1] Many organizations and communities across the nation have also undertaken projects that will enhance our understanding of the Underground Railroad and its implications for contemporary race relations.[2] But considerable misinformation exists, making it difficult to achieve a clear understanding of this secret route to freedom.

What is known with some certainty is that the Underground Railroad began in the early nineteenth century as a clandestine movement to help African American slaves escape from bondage in the South to freedom in the North. Adopting the vocabulary of the railroad, this secret, or "underground," passage to freedom consisted of a loosely organized network of abolitionists who lived in the Southern border states and in the North and assisted fugitives. "Stationmasters" fed and sheltered runaways in their homes, or "stations," while "conductors" guided fugitives between stations.[3]

At the most liberal estimate, some one hundred thousand slaves of the almost four million in bondage escaped on this secret passage.[4] They passed information about methods of escape by word of mouth, in stories, and through songs like "Follow the Drinking Gourd." Often traveling by night, fugitives took advantage of the natural protections offered by swamps, bayous, forests, and waterways. Those traveling in the East often headed to Florida or to such cities as Philadelphia, New York, and Boston. Others fled to Ohio, Illinois, and Michigan. Some fugitives continued on to Canada, where slavery was outlawed and where officials refused U.S. requests for their return.[5]

Whether runaways, stationmasters, or conductors, participants on the Underground Railroad were both black and white, male and female, free and

1

enslaved. They also came from a variety of economic backgrounds, political persuasions, and religious faiths, reflecting the fact that this movement was based, more than anything else, on individual conscience.[6]

As a former schoolteacher and museum educator, I understand the tremendous potential the Underground Railroad possesses to bridge a seemingly distant past with present-day concerns about the moral education of our students. Like the topic of slavery itself, the Underground Railroad and its legacy are critical to understanding America's national character and the responsibility of the individual in the face of social injustice. How, for example, did whites and free blacks reconcile their involvement, or noninvolvement, in a movement that was, according to civil law, illegal? In what ways did race affect the enslaved black person's identity and his relationships to the free black community, the larger white community, and the fundamental institutions of democracy? Does the rhetoric of our country's professed ideals match the reality of government policy? How do we explain our country's failures as well as successes to future generations so they can learn and grow from that understanding?

These are some of the questions that make the Underground Railroad such a complicated as well as fascinating story. They also pique the intellectual curiosity of students, who are often eager to address issues of community conflict and moral decision making.

Educators are always looking for ways to make a personal connection to history for their students, but they do not always have the knowledge or interpretive materials to do it on their own. Both public and scholarly historians recognize this need when it comes to the Underground Railroad.[7]

The purpose of this book is to offer teachers a better understanding of the history, operation, and folklore of the Underground Railroad as well as some engaging lesson plans, simulation exercises, and activities that will allow their students to have a rewarding experience with this important chapter of American history. Although the book was written for middle school teachers—specifically those who teach grades 5, 6, 7, and 8—elementary and high school teachers, museum educators, and instructors of teacher education programs will find that it is easy to adapt the materials provided here to their own age-appropriate curricula. The material, strategies, and class exercises have been successfully used with both younger and older students and, with some minor adjustments on the teachers' part, have proven to be just as challenging, rigorous, and engaging for elementary and high school students as for middle schoolers.

The research, interpretation, and activities contained in the following pages were originally designed for an interactive exhibition I curated at the Chester County Historical Society. Titled *Just Over the Line: Chester County and the Underground Railroad*, the exhibit examined the Underground Railroad's Eastern Line, which ran through Chester County, Pennsylvania, and into Philadelphia.

One of the most rewarding parts of this initiative was working directly with students from public, private, parochial, and special needs schools in the southeastern Pennsylvania region. The educators on staff had specific goals in mind as we developed the curriculum for the exhibit. The goals we had for each and every student were both content- and skill-related:

Content-Related Goals

1. Once a fugitive crossed over the Mason-Dixon Line to the free states of the North, he did not necessarily escape danger. Federal law still upheld the right of the slaveholder to reclaim his slave property, and many did so with the active assistance of Northerners.

2. The story of the Underground Railroad is a fascinating mix of fact and fiction, integrating traditional history with folklore.

3. Involvement on the Underground Railroad was a matter of individual choice, transcending religious, racial, ethnic, gender, and age boundaries, and as such, offers a model for addressing race relations today.

Skill-Related Goals

1. *Critical thinking:* To be able to distinguish fact from folklore; to determine which sources of information are credible; and to understand how to evaluate those sources.

2. *Multiple intelligence–based learning:* To be able to use the different intelligences, including visual, auditory, kinesthetic, and musical intelligences.[8]

3. *Empathy building:* To develop empathy for the fugitives and for those who risked their own safety to help the runaways secure personal freedom.

Some readers may question how an exhibit-based curriculum can be implemented in a school program, when the artifacts, images, and documents are confined to a museum environment. Or, alternatively, some may wonder how museum educators can create an appropriate curriculum for a school when they teach in a very different environment. The key to our success has been in establishing meaningful, ongoing partnerships with local schools.

Gone are the days when a museum staff led students into the galleries and let the objects and exhibits speak for themselves. Today, the museum is a place with a significant teaching role. Teachers and students are invited to become active participants in learning.

In many museums, collections are more accessible than in the past. Interactive exhibit components are now commonplace in most museums, providing students with a firsthand experience. Innovative approaches to learning are also taking place. Outreach, in the form of lesson plans, traveling trunks, and teacher symposia, has also become standard fare at many museums. At the same time, museums rely on important feedback from school communities.

At the Chester County Historical Society, teacher advisory councils with educators who teach a range of age levels assist in program development. Ongoing partnerships exist in the areas of research paper writing, National History Day competitions, and regular museum visits. Internships also exist for those high school and college students as well as graduate students interested in learning more about the field of museum studies. These partnerships help museum educators create programs that meet the needs of the local community. Accordingly, the activities, materials, and exercises in these pages were tested by museum educators and docents, many of whom are retired or former teachers, with the assistance of schools with which we enjoy regular partnerships. Assessment was completed in three ways: (1) informal observation of the students' experiences; (2) student feedback via surveys; and (3) response evaluation, through student work such as essays and research papers.

The book is divided into five chapters. Chapter 1, "Interpreting the Railroad," offers a concise definition of slavery as a starting point for the study of the secret route to freedom. Next, the traditional interpretation of the Underground Railroad is explored. Important distinctions are made between the mythology, fact, and folklore of the movement. The section ends with some important suggestions on how to do research and provides teachers with a useful framework in which to place the activities given in the next four chapters of the book.

Chapter 2, "Documenting the Railroad," explores student interpretation of primary source documents—public declarations, diaries, newspaper advertisements, and letters—related to the Underground Railroad as well as assessment of that work. Chapter 3, "Imagining the Railroad," examines nineteenth-century photographs and engravings of the Underground Railroad and assesses student interpretations of them. The process of writing a local history research paper on an Underground Railroad station and/or agent is the subject of Chapter 4, "Writing the Railroad." Student work as well as assessment and procedural methods are also provided in this section. Chapter 5, "Personalizing the Railroad," offers suggestions on how to pique the curiosity and imaginations of students for the subject through engaging class exercises such as the decoding of letters and escape songs as well as through simulations and living history.

The book closes with an annotated bibliography of books, websites, and educational videos on the Underground Railroad. Collectively, the interpretive material, lesson plans, activities, and resources will allow you to create a living history class for your students as you explore this important chapter in American history.

Endnotes

1. In 1997, President Bill Clinton initiated a national dialogue on race, something he considered to be the "most pressing social issue in our nation today." Convening a presidential commission on race chaired by historian John Hope Franklin, Mr. Clinton wanted to address such issues as affirmative action, reparations for slavery, and the culture of poverty in which so many people of color live.

2. Among the initiatives are the National Underground Railroad Freedom Center, a $110 million museum and educational facility, which opened along Cincinnati's revitalized waterfront in the summer of 2004; the building of a new $12.6 million Liberty Bell Center at Philadelphia's Independence National Historical Park that interprets the complex and simultaneous rise of freedom and of slavery in America; living history programs on slavery and the Underground Railroad at open-air museums like Colonial Williamsburg and Monticello in Virginia and Conner Prairie in Indianapolis; and an educational partnership between Millersville University of Pennsylvania, local historical societies, local school districts, and the Pennsylvania Historical and Museum Commission to develop and integrate an interdisciplinary approach to the Underground Railroad into school curricula. For more information about the many Underground Railroad initiatives that are underway, contact the National Underground Railroad Freedom Center, 50 East Freedom Way, Cincinnati, Ohio 45202. Phone: (513) 333-7500. Website: *www.freedomcenter.org/*.

3. See Charles L. Blockson, *The Underground Railroad* (New York: Berkeley Books, 1987), 1–4; and William J. Switala, *Underground Railroad in Pennsylvania* (Mechanicsburg, PA: Stackpole, 2001), 110–13.

4. Wilbur Siebert, *The Underground Railroad: From Slavery to Freedom* (New York: Macmillan, 1898; reprint, Russell and Russell, 1967), 341.

5. Charles L. Blockson, "Escape from Slavery: The Underground Railroad," *National Geographic* (July 1984): 39.

6. C. Peter Ripley, *The Underground Railroad* (Washington, DC: United States Department of the Interior/National Park Service, 1998), 45–46.

7. See Kim Harris and Reggie Harris, "A View from the Drinking Gourd," *Magazine of History of the Organization of American Historians* (Winter 2002): 16–18; Adam Goodheart, "The Bonds of History," *Preservation* (September/October 2001): 36–43, 94; James O. Horton, "Presenting Slavery: The Perils of Telling America's Racial Story," *The Public Historian* (Fall 1999): 19–38; Kendra Hamilton, "Reinterpreting America's History," *Black Issues in Higher Education* (August 5, 1999): 20–25; and

National Park Service, *Exploring a Common Past: Researching and Interpreting the Underground Railroad* (Washington, DC: Department of the Interior/National Park Service, 1998).

8. See Howard Gardner, *Frames of Mind: A Theory of Multiple Intelligences* (New York: Penguin, 1983). Hailed by educators throughout the world, Gardner's theory of multiple intelligences has been applied in hundreds of classrooms and school districts since *Frames of Mind* was first published in 1983. Gardner challenges the widely held notion that intelligence is a single general capacity possessed by every individual to a greater or lesser extent. Amassing a wealth of evidence, Gardner posits the existence of a number of intelligences that ultimately yield a unique cognitive profile for each person.

Chapter One

Interpreting the Railroad
Providing Students with Context

The information in Chapter 1 offers teachers a succinct overview of slavery and the history, operation, and folklore of the Underground Railroad. It is *not* intended as a definitive treatment of either subject. For those teachers interested in learning more about either subject, I suggest consulting the titles listed in the bibliography under the heading "Readings for Teachers."

The information in this section will also be useful for students as they begin their study of the Underground Railroad. Teachers may want to photocopy and distribute these pages to students when introducing a particular exercise provided in the subsequent parts of this book. For example, students interpreting the 1688 Germantown Protest in Chapter 2 will find the information under "Separating Myth from Reality" in this section useful in understanding the motives and various levels of involvement and noninvolvement of Quakers in the antislavery movement. Similarly, those students analyzing the 1863 photograph of Gordon, a runaway slave, in Chapter 3 will want to read "Slave Families and Their Treatment by Owners" in this section. By doing so, they will have a context for that image as well as a possible explanation for it.

The material in Chapter 1 can also help students in writing their own living history impersonations and in playing their roles more effectively in the simulation exercises provided in Chapter 5. In short, the history presented here offers both teachers and students a useful context to understand and utilize the exercises provided in the rest of the book.

Defining the Underground Railroad

The Underground Railroad was a pseudonym for the clandestine movement of African American slaves escaping out of the South to a loosely organized network of abolitionists who assisted them in their search for freedom in the North. While the enterprise began sometime after 1780 with the gradual abolition of slavery in Pennsylvania, the Underground Railroad was most active between 1835 and 1865. Those abolitionists who operated the secret route adopted the vocabulary of the railroad to disguise its illegal activity. Accordingly, the term *underground* suggested a secret, and *railroad* suggested a method of transportation. Those who opened their homes to runaways were referred to as *stationmasters*, and their homes, *stations*. Others who guided fugitives between stations were called *conductors*. *Stockholders* played a less dangerous—and less conspicuous—role, but one that was extremely important. They provided the finances needed for bribes, transportation, food, and clothing. *Agent* was a more generic term, referring to *anyone* who worked on the Underground Railroad.[1]

Most often, runaways escaped to the North using a loose network of routes through the Southern border states. Two of the most heavily traveled routes were the Eastern and Mid-Western Lines (see Figure 1–1). The Eastern Line originated in Maryland and extended through Pennsylvania into New York or New England and on to Canada. Runaways using the Eastern Line often headed to such cities as Philadelphia, New York, and Boston with the hope of becoming part of the free black community. Some fugitives stowed away on ships and escaped up the coast with the hope of arriving in either Massachusetts or Maine, which were both free states. Others continued on to Canada. The Mid-Western Line, on the other hand, originated in southwestern Ohio, attracting slaves from the Deep South as well as the Upper South states of Kentucky and Tennessee. This route took fugitives across the Ohio River to a number of routes through Ohio, Indiana, and Illinois into Canada, where officials refused U.S. requests for their return.[2]

Slavery in America

Any study of the Underground Railroad must begin by addressing the institution of slavery. Slavery was the reason for the creation of the Underground Railroad. An ancient system of labor and property relationships, whereby one person owned another, slavery was originally a byproduct of war and conquest, which required physical brutality for organization.[3]

The systematic exploitation of the West African coast as a source of slaves accompanied the naval explorations of Spain, Portugal, the Netherlands, and Britain. During the fifteenth, sixteenth, seventeenth, and eighteenth centuries, these countries created a slave trade that brought thousands of blacks in chains to South and North America and the Caribbean islands.

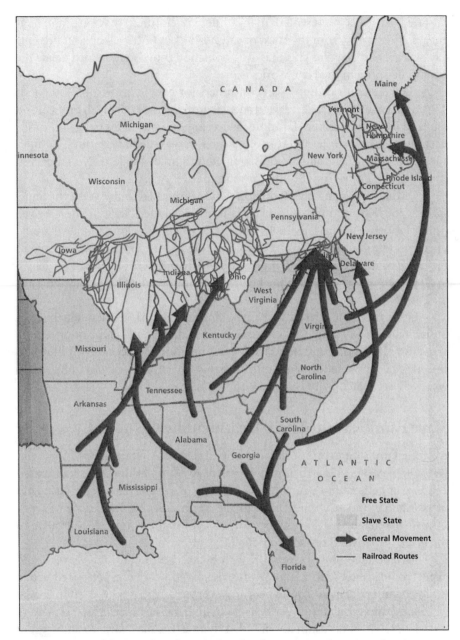

Figure 1–1. *Map of national Underground Railroad routes, 1860 (Just Over the Line exhibit, Chester County Historical Society, West Chester, Pennsylvania)*

Enslaved Africans represented many different cultures, religions, and languages. Most came from the coast or interior of West Africa, between present-day Senegal and Angola. This massive population movement helped create the African diaspora in the New World.

The demands of European consumers for New World crops and goods helped fuel the slave trade. Slave traders from Holland, Portugal, France, and England followed a triangular route, delivering Africans in exchange for products such as rum, sugar, and tobacco, which were in demand among Europeans. Eventually, the trade also distributed Virginian tobacco, New England rum, and rice crops from South Carolina and Georgia.[4]

Of the approximately 10 million Africans shipped to the Western Hemisphere, 450,000 were taken to what is now the United States.[5] They arrived primarily between the late 1600s and 1808, when the United States banned the importation of slaves from Africa. Captured Africans were transported in the holds of ships designed to utilize every inch of space for human cargo. Up to 20 percent did not survive the horrible oceanic journey known as the Middle Passage.

Once the ship arrived in North America, the Africans might be sold individually at any ship dock. Posters in all major U.S. ports announced the arrival of slave ships and advertised auctions. Auctions continued after the end of legal importation, and a great many African American family members were separated from each other.

Slave Families and Their Treatment by Owners

A strong family and community life helped sustain African Americans in slavery. People often chose their own partners, lived under the same roof, raised children together, and protected each other by inventing passive strategies of resistance and teaching them to the young. Techniques such as work slowdowns, feigned sickness, and even self-mutilation were all indicative of the black initiative to resist slavery.[6]

Slaveholders often responded with brutal treatment. Male slaves could expect to be lashed with a leather whip. Enslaved women experienced sexual exploitation at the hands of owners and overseers. Those who tried to escape were sometimes forced to wear bells on their arms, neck, or head. Some were muzzled. Owners occasionally branded their slaves like cattle to show proof of their ownership.[7] Such cruel treatment, designed to instill humility and submission in the slave as well as to extract more work, was a major factor for many slaves in their decision to run away. Other reasons included the death of a master, which caused great fear and apprehension among slaves about their own future as well as the future of their families; escaping the sexual advances of white masters; and, above all, the desire to be reunited with family members.[8]

Beginnings of the Antislavery Movement

Slavery existed in both the North and the South in the seventeenth century and throughout most of the eighteenth century. Pennsylvania, however, became one of the first northern states to provide for the abolition of slavery in 1780 when the state legislature passed the Gradual Abolition Act. While the new law did not free those enslaved at the time, it did provide for the gradual manumission, or the freeing of those slaves born after March 1, 1780, after they reached the age of twenty-eight.[9] Pennsylvania, now a "free state," quickly became a popular destination point for runaway slaves. After the American Revolution, most northern states embraced gradual abolition with the adoption of new state constitutions. Additionally, the first national Congress, in 1787, passed the Northwest Ordinance, which prohibited slavery in the territories west of the Ohio River. Ohio, Indiana, Illinois, Michigan, and Wisconsin were carved out of this region and also became popular points of destination for fugitive slaves.[10]

Generally, both northerners and southerners believed that slavery was a moral evil and that, in time, the issue would resolve itself. But the introduction of the cotton gin in 1793 made slave labor essential to the success of the southern economy, making slavery not only the "peculiar institution" of that region but a cherished way of life. To protect the property rights of the slaveholders, the federal Congress passed the Fugitive Slave Law in 1793, requiring all citizens to assist in the recapture of a runaway slave or face severe fines and/or imprisonment. With the admission of Missouri to the union as a slave state in 1820, slavery became, as Thomas Jefferson warned, "a firebell in the night" for the nation.[11] The so-called Missouri Compromise allowed slavery to expand into the western territories, south of 36° 30' latitude. By 1860, a new social hierarchy based on slave ownership had developed in the South. Of the 1,516,000 free families who lived in that region, there were 385,000 slaveholders. Depending upon the number of slaves a family owned, it belonged to one of the following groups:[12]

> *Planter aristocracy:* Composed less than 1 percent of the South's free population; this small minority of 3,000 families owned more than 100 slaves each.

> *Large planters:* Composed less than 1 percent of the South's free population; this group of 10,000 families owned between 50 and 100 slaves each.

Small planters: Composed approximately 6 percent of the South's free population; this group of 102,000 families owned between 10 and 50 slaves each.

Independent white farmers: Composed approximately 18 percent of the South's free population; this group of 270,000 families owned fewer than 10 slaves each.

Non-slaveholders: The majority of white Southerners—about 75 percent, or 1,131,000 families—owned no slaves at all.

Despite the relatively small numbers of slaveholders, the nation's growing demands for cotton and sugar made the peculiar institution a self-sustaining one. In 1840 cotton exports exceeded all others combined by almost 52 percent. Two decades later, in 1860, the value of slaves exceeded the value of all railroads, banks, and factories combined.[13] Widespread concern emerged over the future of a rapidly expanding country, namely whether the United States would become a modern, industrial society based on free labor like the North, or a more traditional agrarian society based on slave labor like the South. Northern abolitionists also raised a concern over the morality of slavery. The most radical abolitionists, determined to end this infamous practice, disobeyed civil law by banding together as active agents on the Underground Railroad.

Separating Myth from Reality

Because the Underground Railroad operated in secrecy and has few remaining records, it is shrouded in 150 years of mythology. Many of the most basic facts about its history and operation are unknown. No one knows, for example, how many fugitives successfully fled from bondage along its invisible tracks. Nor is there any reliable source for the origins of the term *Underground Railroad;* all we have are educated guesses based largely on anecdotal information handed down across the generations. According to one legend, the name originated in 1831 when a Kentucky master was tracking one of his own slaves who had escaped. The slave, Tice Davids, made it across the Ohio River with his master in hot pursuit. Once on the other side, however, the master lost all trace of the runaway and supposedly declared that his slave must have "gone off on an underground railroad."[14]

Traditionally, the mythology emphasizes a free North and a slaveholding South. It assumes that white abolitionist operators were unified in their opposition to slavery and credits them with the success of the clandestine enterprise, while fugitives are depicted as helpless, frightened passengers, who took advantage of a well-organized national network. These misconceptions stem, in part, from the lack of reliable sources as well as the unconventional use of those that do exist. Many accounts were written years after the fact by white abolitionists, who tended to emphasize their own heroics and omit the contributions of others, most notably the free black community and the fugitives themselves. Often these accounts were further embellished and replicated in subsequent novels, plays, and, in some cases, historical monographs like R. C. Smedley's *History of the Underground Railroad in Chester and the Neighboring Counties* (1883) and Wilbur H. Siebert's *Underground Railroad from Slavery to Freedom* (1898). The result was an overemphasis on white abolitionist involvement, particularly among Quakers, and an oversimplification of a complex historical phenomenon that involved many religious groups as well as free blacks and fugitives themselves.[15]

To be sure, Quakers were not the only religious group to participate in the Underground Railroad, but they were the best known. As early as 1688, the Quakers of Germantown Meeting, near Philadelphia, drafted the first antislavery petition in America. Acting on the Friends' most fundamental belief of an Inner Light, or the presence of God in every human being, the Germantown Friends reasoned that if God manifested His presence in each individual, then, in His eyes, all humans were of equal value, regardless of race. Accordingly, they urged their Quaker brethren to "stand against the practice of bringing slaves to this country, or selling them against their own will."[16]

In 1759, Philadelphia Yearly Meeting, the governing body of Friends in southeastern Pennsylvania, forbade members to continue any involvement in the slave trade.[17] Seventeen years later, in 1776, slaveholding was made a cause for disownment within the Religious Society of Friends.[18] Afterward, individual Friends shifted their antislavery campaign to the larger, non-Quaker society by appealing to the moral conscience of those who held slaves.

It is important to note, however, that not all Quakers were abolitionists and certainly not all were Underground Railroad agents. In fact, divisions over theology, social reform, and politics among Friends in Indiana led to the establishment of a separate Indiana Yearly Meeting of Antislavery Friends in 1842. A similar split occurred in Pennsylvania between the Philadelphia Yearly Meeting and a schismatic group called the Pennsylvania Yearly Meeting of Progressive Friends in 1853. Several members of both splinter groups were active Underground Railroad agents.[19] Among the most noted were Levi Coffin of Cincinnati; Thomas Garrett of Wilmington, Delaware; and Lucretia Mott of Philadelphia.

The Presbyterian, Baptist, and Methodist Churches were divided over the issue of slavery. Often the divisions occurred along regional lines, with Southern congregations advocating slavery and Northern ones opposing it. Those congregations who opposed the peculiar institution operated on the belief that the principles of Christianity, as set forth in the Bible, compelled them to act against it. Their understanding of a "higher law," which superceded federal law, resulted in antislavery involvements that ran the gamut from colonization, or the resettlement of former slaves to Africa, to active participation in the Underground Railroad. It is important to note, however, that for any church to openly affiliate itself with an illegal movement like the Underground Railroad would be to incriminate itself and its congregants. Nevertheless, *individual* members of several white denominations participated in the secret route to freedom, including the Universalists, Mennonites, Moravians, Lutherans, Anglicans, and Disciples of Christ.[20] Few of their Underground Railroad efforts, however, would have been achieved without the active help of the free black community.

Charles Blockson has identified the aggressive and sustained Underground Railroad activity of African Americans and the African Methodist Episcopal Church. Because of the common bonds of blood and culture, the free black community was much more empathetic than any white denomination with the circumstances of their enslaved brethren and, hence, more aggressive in their antislavery activities than white agents. There was never any question in the minds of blacks about the evils of slavery, the need to abolish it as quickly as possible, or the moral obligation to assist runaways.[21] James and Lois Horton have also written important works on the Northern free black community and its relationship with white abolitionists. Their research reveals a multifaceted and pluralistic free black society in southeastern Pennsylvania. While disagreement over leadership styles existed in that community, it did not preclude cooperation toward common goals within the free black community or with the white abolitionist community, particularly in such areas as abolitionism, involvement with the Underground Railroad, and securing educational opportunities for African Americans.[22]

The most balanced treatment of the clandestine route to freedom, however, is William Still's *Underground Railroad*, which continues to be widely considered by historians as the most accurate source on the topic. Still, a free black abolitionist and chairman of the Pennsylvania Antislavery Society's Vigilance Committee, personally interviewed fugitives who came under his protection. He recorded their personal histories: where they came from, who their masters were, how they escaped, why they escaped, and the dangers they encountered on their flight to freedom. Still carefully guarded the interviews until 1872, when he integrated his own observations as well as personal correspondence, excerpts from newspaper articles, minutes of antislavery meetings, and legal papers, and published them in an eight-hundred-page book.[23]

Unlike many of his contemporaries, Still credited white abolitionists, free black people, and fugitives with the success of the Underground Railroad. "As a general rule," he wrote, "the passengers of the Underground Railroad were physically and intellectually above the average order of slaves and were determined to have liberty even at the cost of life." Such fugitives as Henry "Box" Brown, who freighted himself to freedom in a wooden crate, and Ellen and William Craft, who ingeniously disguised themselves as a slave master and servant and traveled by train and boat from the Deep South to Philadelphia, were not helpless individuals but very capable, self-reliant people who took matters into their own hands and, in so doing, impressed Still. At the same time, Still acknowledged the "Christ-like exhibition of love and humanity" extended by white abolitionists such as Thomas Garrett, Lucretia Mott, and William Lloyd Garrison, "who served the antislavery cause in its darkest days."[24] Still reminds us that involvement on the Underground Railroad was an *individual* decision based on moral choice, and one that transcended the boundaries of religion, race, socioeconomics, gender, and age.

Interracial cooperation was key to the success of the enterprise and the primary reason that the Underground Railroad is popularly evoked as a historical model for contemporary race relations. For example, Harriet Tubman, the most famous conductor on the Underground Railroad, was a frequent visitor to the home of white Quaker Thomas Garrett. She alone is credited with conducting more than three hundred people out of bondage, earning the reputation of the "Moses of her people."[25] Garrett also relied heavily on other free black conductors such as Severen Johnson, Comegeys Munson, and Joseph Hamilton.[26] Between 1830 and 1860, some nine thousand runaways were guided to freedom through the Eastern Line because of the joint efforts of Quakers and blacks in general, and because of the individual efforts of William Still and Garrett in particular.[27]

At the same time, there were ideological and tactical differences between white and black abolitionists that sometimes broke into open conflict. For example, William Lloyd Garrison, the white editor of the abolitionist newspaper *Liberator* and leading advocate of immediate emancipation, parted ways over policy with Frederick Douglass, the free black editor of the *North Star* and a prominent antislavery orator. Garrison discouraged Douglass from having any active participation in planning abolitionist strategies, preferring that he limit his role to speaking about the evils of slavery. Expressing his appreciation for Garrison's antislavery commitment, Douglass told the white abolitionist editor that it was time for "those of us who suffered the wrong to lead the way in advocating liberty." Infuriated by the rebuff, Garrison tried to prevent Douglass from publishing the *North Star* and later discredited him as an abolitionist leader.[28] Nor were Quaker abolitionists, noted for their pacifist beliefs, very happy with Douglass when, after the passage of the Fugitive Slave Law of 1850, he argued the "rightfulness of forcible resistance." Urging free blacks to arm themselves, Douglass insisted that the "only way to make the Fugitive Slave Law a dead letter is to make a half dozen or more dead kidnappers."[29] Similar disputes broke out between black abolitionists Henry Bibb and William Wells Brown and white abolitionists who worked with them.[30]

These conflicts can be attributed to the fact that whites tended to see abolitionism in abstract terms. It was tied to the abridgment of constitutional rights or, theologically, to the violation of a higher law doctrine. Blacks, on the other hand, saw abolitionism, like slavery, in much more personal terms. It involved the ability to hold families together, for a husband and wife to live in the same household, to determine their own future as well as the future of their children, and to enjoy the same God-given rights as any white person.[31] When white abolitionists began to think about the more practical considerations of their antislavery involvement, it provoked fears of assimilation, or worse, miscegenation. Thus, while white abolitionists might have been progressive enough to challenge the moral conventions of antebellum society that condoned slavery—and even worked together with blacks in the effort to achieve emancipation—their inability to transcend the racism of their society inevitably defined them as products of it. This is not to say that white abolitionists were hypocrites, but rather that even the antislavery movement had its social limits.

Another myth that has clouded the history of the Underground Railroad is the degree to which the enterprise was organized. Because of the popular focus on the white contribution and the Quakers' reputation for close-knit associations in their social and economic involvements, historians have generally described a highly organized movement. In fact, organization was largely restricted to a few rural areas and, in the 1840s, to Northern cities like Boston, New York, and Philadelphia, where vigilance committees arose to combat the increasing threat posed by the federal government's enforcement of fugitive slave laws.[32] Especially after 1850, fugitives were not safe once they crossed over the Mason-Dixon Line because the new Fugitive Slave Law required bystanders to assist the authorities and made the legal process simpler for slave catchers as they plied their trade. Under these circumstances the border regions dividing the free and slave states became battlegrounds in the struggle between disgruntled Southern slave owners and Northern abolitionists.

To combat the success of the Underground Railroad, a second fugitive slave act was passed by Congress in 1850. This measure strengthened the 1793 law by mandating the recapture and extradition of escaped slaves. It also levied fines and prison sentences on individuals who helped runaways and on those who refused to assist in their recapture.[33] The law resulted in an increase in the kidnapping of free blacks by unscrupulous traders, greater immigration to Canada, and violent resistance by many free black communities.[34]

By 1860, a growing rift between the free states and the slave states was determining the future of the country. Would the United States become a modern nation based on free labor, or would it continue to depend on slave labor? Shortly after Abraham Lincoln, an opponent of slavery, became president in 1861, the South seceded from the union and it was clear that the issue of slavery would be decided by civil war.

With the North's victory and the adoption of the Thirteenth Amendment to the U.S. Constitution in 1865, slavery was abolished and the Underground Railroad was no more.

Folklore

The folklore of the Underground Railroad presents a more complicated issue than the mythology, especially since the two are often confused. *Mythology*, properly defined, is any fictitious or imaginary story about the origins or history of a people. It is based more on tradition or convenience than fact. *Folklore*, on the other hand, is the oral culture and traditions of a people, consisting of customs, pastimes, songs, stories, and material culture.[35] It is grounded in fact and often presented in tangible objects, such as arts and crafts. To be sure, some of the folklore associated with the Underground Railroad is embellished, being spun from popular anecdotes designed to boost the pride of a small-town community. Under these circumstances, exaggerated accounts of daring rescues, ingenious hiding places, and great escapes have become accepted fact, though they are not documented.

While folklore and oral testimonies are sometimes controversial because they lack corroboration in written documentation, these sources are central to the African American experience and must be addressed in any examination of the Underground Railroad. Because most slaves could not read or write, they were dependent on oral testimonies to tell their history. Additionally, storytelling was fundamentally important to most African cultures as a method of transmitting their history across generations.[36]

Middle school students, in particular, are often fascinated with folklore because it sparks their imaginations. Quilts, for example, were believed to be used as a covert method of communication to aid runaways in their escape though no primary source documentation exists to support this popular belief.[37] There is, however, significant evidence that spirituals and popular slave songs contained codes. "Follow the Drinking Gourd" directed slaves to follow a particular route of escape by way of the North Star. Similarly, "Go Down, Moses," announced the arrival of conductor Harriet Tubman, the so-called Moses of her people, and an impending escape.[38]

Naturally, student research on the topic of the Underground Railroad must be grounded in primary source documentation: contemporary newspaper accounts; personal correspondence; daily journals; maps; images and photographs; records of antislavery societies, vigilance committees, and churches; and legal documents and court records. But the research may also draw on the stories, anecdotes, and folklore that have been passed down through the generations, especially if those stories come from African American families. While every effort should be made to distinguish the oral history from the documented material, both are critical to a multicultural understanding of the Underground Railroad.

Suggestions for Interpretation

Responsible historical interpretation of the Underground Railroad is grounded in careful, thoughtful research that draws on a variety of primary and secondary sources. Here are some useful suggestions:

1. *Provide context:* Be sure to begin your study of the Underground Railroad by giving students sufficient background information so that they understand the significance of the movement to the institutions of slavery and abolitionism as well as its relationship to important events like the Civil War.

2. *Define your terms carefully:* Be clear on the origins, operation, and effects of the Underground Railroad when you introduce the subject. Identify and separate the myths and legends from historical facts about the movement.

3. *Present a balanced view:* The history of the Underground Railroad can be told from a variety of perspectives. For some, it was a story of strength and survival. For others, it was a painful farewell to family and friends. Still others viewed the secret route to freedom as an intrusion of their rights as property holders, or a way to make money at the misfortune of runaways. Whether a slave owner, kidnapper, stationmaster, conductor, or runaway, every participant had a perspective. Be sure to address them all. The Underground Railroad's complexity is part of the popular fascination with the subject. Avoid the simple answer when explaining the subject.

4. *Enliven the interpretation:* Don't lecture at students; engage them. Be sure to include singing, arts and crafts, movies, living history, simulation exercises, as well as oral history in presenting the Underground Railroad. Some examples follow in Chapter 5.

5. *Visit the site in person or on the Web:* If you are aware of a documented Underground Railroad station in your area, plan a class trip or encourage

students to visit the site. If your school is located in a geographic area that wasn't part of the Underground Railroad, tap into one of the websites provided in the bibliography. Some of these websites have virtual tours of stations once used on the Underground Railroad. Learning by doing is always preferable to book learning for youngsters. Prepare a worksheet with specific questions for your students. Be sure that the questions range from the concrete (e.g., When was the structure built? Who lived in it? Describe its physical features) to the abstract (e.g., Why do you think the owner participated in the Underground Railroad?).

6. *Make contemporary connections:* Any historical movement is made more meaningful if it has personal relevance for a student. The Underground Railroad is especially fascinating because it was based on successful interracial cooperation, something we promote in our own multicultural society. Capitalize on the opportunity to relate the Underground Railroad to current-events issues such as affirmative action, reparations, and racial profiling. By doing so, you will register the important point that the search for historical truth is ongoing and can be shaped by the social and moral conventions of the present.

Summary

Any interpretation of the Underground Railroad must begin with an investigation of slavery itself. Only then will students understand the motivations of a runaway slave and the human element involved in the story of the Underground Railroad.

Just as important is integrating the folklore of the movement into that story. To be sure, documentary evidence is vital to our understanding of the Underground Railroad and should be used whenever available. But limiting the story to written documentation confines it primarily to the perspective of an educated white elite.

Students must understand that African culture emphasized oral tradition and folklore—not the written word—and that those methods are also viable forms of explaining the past. The telling of history through oral tradition and folklore continued in the United States, where African American slaves, deprived of an education, communicated their stories through word of mouth, in songs, and through apocryphal stories that made up the folklore of the slave community.

Such a multicultural and interdisciplinary approach will not only give students a greater understanding of the Underground Railroad and the important roles played by free blacks and the runaways themselves but also cultivate an appreciation for African American culture.

Endnotes

1. John Hope Franklin, *From Slavery to Freedom: A History of Negro Americans*. (New York: Alfred A. Knopf, 1980, 5th ed.), 189–94; James A. McGowan, *Station Master on the Underground Railroad: The Life and Letters of Thomas Garrett* (Moylan, PA: Whimsie, 1977), 5.

2. C. Peter Ripley, *The Underground Railroad* (Washington, DC: United States Department of the Interior/National Park Service, 1998), 48, 54.

3. Franklin, *From Slavery to Freedom*, 34–35; Kenneth M. Stampp, *The Peculiar Institution: Slavery in the Ante-Bellum South* (New York: Vintage, 1956), 4–6.

4. See Hugh Thomas, *The Slave Trade* (New York: Simon and Schuster, 1997).

5. Peter J. Parish, *Slavery: History and Historians* (New York: Harper, 1989), 12.

6. See Eugene Genovese, *Roll Jordan, Roll: The World the Slaves Made* (New York: Pantheon, 1974); John W. Blassingame, *The Slave Community: Plantation Life in the Antebellum South* (New York: Oxford University, 1972); and Leslie H. Owens, *This Species of Property: Slave Life and Culture in the Old South* (New York: Oxford University Press, 1976).

7. See Eugene Genovese, *The World the Slaveholders Made* (New York: Pantheon, 1969).

8. John Hope Franklin and Loren Schweninger, *Runaway Slaves: Rebels on the Plantation* (New York: Oxford University Press, 1999), 7–48.

9. Gary B. Nash and Jean R. Soderlund, *Freedom by Degrees: Emancipation in Pennsylvania and Its Aftermath* (New York: Oxford University Press, 1991), 119.

10. Don E. Fehrenbacher, *The Slaveholding Republic: An Account of the United States Government's Relation to Slavery* (New York: Oxford University Press, 2001), 203–08.

11. Sarah Amsler, *Exploring a Common Past: Researching and Interpreting the Underground Railroad* (Washington, DC: Department of the Interior/National Park Service, 1998), 8.

12. See *Decennial Records* (Washington, DC: United States Bureau of the Census, 1860).

13. James O. Horton quoted in *Whispers of Angels: A Story of the Underground Railroad* (Wilmington, DE: Teleduction educational film documentary, 2002).

14. Franklin, *From Slavery to Freedom*, 190; Larry Gara, "Some Lessons from the Underground Railroad," in *New Historical Perspectives: Essays on the Black Experience in Antebellum America*, ed. Gene Lewis (Cincinnati: Cincinnati Historical Society, 1984), 39; and Carol Kammen, "The Underground Railroad and Local History," *History News* (Spring 1999): 3.

15. For secondary source accounts that exaggerate the events of the Underground Railroad, see Wilbur H. Siebert, *The Underground Railroad from Slavery to Freedom* (1898) (New York: Arno, 1968 reprint); R. C. Smedley, *History of the Under-*

ground Railroad in Chester and the Neighboring Counties (Lancaster, PA: 1883); and Sarah H. Bradford, *Scenes in the Life of Harriet Tubman* (Auburn, NY: W. J. Moses, 1869). For primary source accounts, see Levi Coffin, *Reminiscences of Levi Coffin: The Reputed President of the Underground Railroad* (Cincinnati: Robert Clarke, 1876); and Alexander M. Ross, *Recollections and Experiences of an Abolitionist* (Toronto: Rowell and Hutchinson, 1875).

16. Francis Daniel Pastorius, "Germantown Protest, 1688," quoted in Thomas E. Drake, *Quakers and Slavery in America* (New Haven: Yale University Press, 1950), 34.

17. Jean Soderlund, *Quakers and Slavery: A Divided Spirit* (Princeton, NJ: Princeton University Press, 1985), 90–92.

18. Philadelphia Yearly Meeting Minutes: 1776; see also Jack Marietta, *The Reformation of American Quakerism, 1748–1783* (Philadelphia: University of Pennsylvania Press, 1984).

19. See Pennsylvania Yearly Meeting of Progressive Friends, *Proceedings, 1853–1878* (West Chester, PA: Chester County Historical Society, 2 vols.); Albert J. Wahl, "The Congregational, or Progressive Friends in the Pre-Civil War Reform Movement" (Ph.D. diss., Temple University, 1951); William C. Kashatus, *Just Over the Line: Chester County (PA) and the Underground Railroad* (West Chester, PA: Chester County Historical Society, 2002), 63–64; Walter Edgerton, *A History of the Separation in Indiana Yearly Meeting of the Society of Friends in the Winter of 1842 and 1843 on the Anti-Slavery Question* (Cincinnati, 1856); Thomas Hamm, "Moral Choices: Two Indiana Quaker Communities and the Abolitionist Movement," *Indiana Magazine of History* (June 1991): 117–54; and Ryan Jordan, "The Indiana Separation of 1842 and the Limits of Quaker Antislavery," *Quaker History* (Spring 2000): 1–27.

20. See William W. Sweet, *The Story of Religion in America* (New York: Harper & Row, 1930), 170–180; David Christy, *Pulpit Politics; or, Ecclesiastical Legislation on Slavery in Its Disturbing Influences on the American Union* (New York: Farran and McLean, 1862); and William Switala, *Underground Railroad in Pennsylvania* (Mechanicsburg, PA: Stackpole, 2001), 165–75.

21. See Charles L. Blockson, *The Underground Railroad in Pennsylvania* (Jacksonville, NC: Flame International, 1981); Charles L. Blockson, "Escape from Slavery: The Underground Railroad," *National Geographic* (July 1984): 39–48; and Charles L. Blockson, *Hippocrene Guide to the Underground Railroad* (New York: Hippocrene, 1994).

22. James O. Horton and Lois E. Horton, *In Hope of Liberty: Culture, Community and Protest Among Northern Free Blacks, 1700–1860* (New York: Oxford University Press, 1997); and James O. Horton and Lois E. Horton, *Black Bostonians: Family Life and Community Struggle in the Antebellum North* (New York: Homes and Meier, 1999, rev. ed.).

23. William Still, *The Underground Railroad* (1872) (Chicago: Johnson, 1970 reprint).

24. Ibid., xiii.

25. Sarah Bradford, *Harriet Tubman: The Moses of Her People* (1886) (Bedford MA: Applewood, 1993 reprint).

26. McGowan, *Station Master,* 96–99.

27. Ripley, *Underground Railroad,* 61.

28. See Henry Mayer, *All on Fire: William Lloyd Garrison and the Abolition of Slavery* (New York: St. Martin's, 1998), 371–74, 431–33; and Gara, "Some Lessons," 43.

29. Frederick Douglass, *My Bondage and My Freedom* (1855), ed. by Philip S. Foner (New York: Dover, 1969 reprint), 454–456.

30. Gara, "Some Lessons," 43.

31. Ibid.

32. Ibid., 42.

33. "Fugitive Slave Law of 1850," in Henry Steele Commager, ed., *Documents of American History* (New York: Appleton-Century-Crofts, 1986), 321–23.

34. Franklin, *From Slavery to Freedom,* 200.

35. See Don Yoder, *Discovering American Folklife* (Mechanicsburg, PA: Stackpole, 2001), 27.

36. For works on oral tradition and African American culture, see Linda Goss and Clay Goss, *Jump Up and Say: A Collection of Black Storytelling* (New York: Simon and Schuster, 1995); Virginia Hamilton, *The People Could Fly: American Black Folktales* (New York: Alfred A. Knopf, 1985); and Nancy Roan and Donald Roan, *Lest I Shall Be Forgotten: Anecdotes and Traditions of Quilts* (Green Lane, PA: Goschenhoppen Historians, 1993).

37. Some folklorists believe that quilt codes, done in geometric patterns and distinctive stitchings, were used to aid slaves in memorizing certain directives before their escape. Specific names, which functioned as metaphors in the code, were assigned to various quilt patterns. If a "Monkey Wrench" quilt pattern was being displayed, for example, slaves knew that they were to gather all the "tools" they would need on an impending escape to the North. A "Wagon Wheel" pattern signified the method of transportation they would take. If a "Tumbling Boxes" pattern appeared, slaves knew that the moment of escape had arrived. See Jacqueline L. Tobin and Raymond G. Dobard, *Hidden in Plain View: A Secret Story of Quilts and the Underground Railroad* (New York: Anchor, 2000), 69–71; For other works on quilt codes, see Roland L. Freeman, *A Communion of the Spirits: African-American Quilters, Preservers, and Their Stories* (Nashville, TN: Rutledge Hill, 1996); Gladys-Marie Fry, "Harriet Powers: Portrait of a Black Quilter," in *Missing Pieces: Georgia Folk Art, 1770–1976,* ed. Anna Wadsworth (Atlanta: Georgia Council of the Arts and Humanities, 1976); Gladys-Marie Fry, *Stitched from the Soul: Slave Quilts from the Antebellum South* (New York: Dutton, 1990); Eva U. Gruden, *Stitching Memories: African-American Story Quilts* (Williamstown, MA: Williams College Museum of Art, 1990); Eli Leon, *Who'd a Thought It: Improvisations in African-American Quiltmaking* (San Francisco: Craft and Folk Art Museum, 1987); Mary E. Lyons, *Stitching Stars: The Story Quilts of Har-*

riet Powers (New York: Charles Scribner's Sons, 1993); Regenia A. Perry, *Harriet Powers's Bible Quilts* (New York: St. Martin's, 1994); and Maude S. Wahlman, *Signs and Symbols: African Images in African-American Quilts* (New York: Studio/Museum of American Folk Art, 1993).

38. For works on escape songs and spirituals, see Harold Courlander, *Negro Folk Music, U.S.A.* (New York: Dover, 1992); Miles M. Fisher, *Negro Slave Songs in the United States* (New York: Citadel, 1968); Samuel A. Floyd Jr., *The Power of Black Music* (New York: Oxford University Press, 1995); and Arthur C. Jones, *Wade in the Water: The Wisdom of the Spirituals* (New York: Orbis, 1993).

Chapter Two

Documenting the Railroad
Teaching with Documents

During the last few years there has been a proliferation of books on the Underground Railroad for students of all ages. In addition, the most recently published U.S. history textbooks now devote greater coverage than ever before to the topic. These secondary sources are wonderful starting points for students as they embark on a study of the Underground Railroad. But primary source documents are the real "stuff" of history and must be integrated into their investigation of the topic.

Documents fascinate middle school students because they are real and they are personal. Teaching with documents allows middle schoolers to touch directly the lives of people in the past. Sometimes that can evoke emotional responses, enabling students to identify with the human factor in history, including the risks, courage, and contradictions of those who shaped the past.

Chapter 2 explores documents—public declarations, diaries, newspaper advertisements, letters—that relate to slavery, abolitionism, and the Underground Railroad. Some are well-known, like the Emancipation Proclamation. Others are less conspicuous sources but still played a significant role among those who embraced abolitionism. The Germantown Protest of 1688, for example, was the first antislavery petition in America and one that stirred individual Quakers to act on their antislavery convictions.

Still other documents are more personal and were not made available to historians until the twentieth century. Among these are the diary of David Evans, a Quaker farmer whose personal reflections offer a detailed description of the routes, participants, and stations on southeastern Pennsylvania's Underground Railroad, and the letters of Thomas Garrett and William Still, stationmasters whose friendship transcended both race and religion, resulting in the passage of more than twenty-seven hundred slaves to freedom. Each one of these documents offers middle school students a different perspective of antebellum culture and the runaways, slaveholders, and abolitionists who shaped it.

Teachers will want to refer to the history given in Chapter 1 to provide themselves and their students with the necessary background they will need to complete the critical thinking and writing exercises in this section. For example, students interpreting a document such as the Emancipation Proclamation will want to read over the history provided in Chapter 1 under the subheading "Beginnings of the Antislavery Movement" in order to understand the kind of pressure President Abraham Lincoln was receiving from abolitionists in 1862 when he decided to emancipate the slaves. To what degree was Lincoln's decision based on that pressure?

Similarly, students interpreting the fugitive slave advertisements in this section will want to read the history given in Chapter 1 under the subheadings "Slavery in America" and "Slave Families and Their Treatment by Owners" in order to understand why the advertisements were written as well as why the slave owner chose to describe the runaway's physical features.

Here are some of the issues students will want to address as they examine the documents. They are also wonderful issues for a class discussion once students complete their document analyses. Can you see any similarities between the two advertisements provided in this chapter? Are the descriptions any different from those of a lost pet? What do the descriptions tell you about the way slaveholders viewed their runaways?

Distinguishing Between Primary and Secondary Sources

A primary source document is any document created by those who participated in or witnessed the events of the past. Newspapers, journals, diaries, government papers, wills, speeches, letters, drawings, engravings, and photographs are examples of primary source documents. Primary sources reflect the personal, social, political, and/or economic views of the participants, who had their own biases and motives in recording their thoughts. These records challenge students to examine their own biases, created by their own personal circumstances and the environments in which they live. Ultimately students come to realize that history is interpretation and that interpreting documents helps them analyze and evaluate contemporary sources, whether they are newspaper accounts, popular magazines, television or radio programs, or Internet sources.

Articles and books, on the other hand, are considered secondary sources written after a historical event, usually ten or more years afterward. Secondary sources are written to describe, analyze, or reconstruct an earlier event. By their very nature, they are secondhand interpretations, subject to the distortions of the time that has elapsed. That doesn't mean they are not useful. Because secondary sources are written years after a historical event, they can provide an extremely helpful perspective and important insight on people, places, and events of the past. In other words, sufficient distance from a historical event affords the contemporary writer a special advantage: he or she can craft his or her own interpretation based on a knowledge of the effects of a particular event or through surveying a wide array of documents about the event. For example, John Hope Franklin and Loren Schweninger's seminal study *Runaway Slaves: Rebels on the Plantation* is an indispensable source for historians, researchers and scholars interested in the Underground Railroad. The book offers readers a groundbreaking analysis of slave resistance and escape, debunking the traditional theory that slaves were generally pliant and resigned to their status as human chattel. Franklin and Schweninger show how slaves resisted and escaped, where they fled to, and how they survived away from the plantation. Their argument is supported by a wealth of documents, including planters' records, petitions to county courts and state legislatures, and local newspapers.

A Model for Analyzing Primary Source Documents

Analyzing primary source documents is not only a valuable exercise for building critical thinking skills, but it also provides students with an essential research tool for writing. In analyzing documents, it is important that students are able to answer six major questions:

What? What kind of document is it? What is the content? The answers to these questions may seem obvious, but the way a document is described actually indicates the student's understanding of it. Students should be able to summarize the most important issues raised by the document and do so by integrating the most relevant quotations into the body of the description.

Who? Who is the author of the document? Students may not always be able to identify the author by name, but they can usually identify other characteristics that may be important to understanding his or her motive for writing the document. They should consider such characteristics as gender, race, ethnicity, and political and religious affiliation.

When? When was the document written? Students should be able to identify not only the date on which the document was written, but also the major events that were occurring at the time. This identification is extremely important in understanding the historical context of the document. For example, a student must know that Harriet Beecher Stowe's work *Uncle*

Tom's Cabin (1852) was written shortly after the passage of the federal government's 1850 Fugitive Slave Law. Without that knowledge, her book becomes less relevant, because it was written in response to that law. Its immediate popularity among abolitionists and the controversy it caused among slaveholders prompted President Lincoln, when he later met Stowe, to remark: "So you're the person whose book started this great [Civil] war!"

Where? Where was the document written? The location may or may not be significant. Lincoln, for example, could have written the Emancipation Proclamation anywhere in the union in 1862 and the document still would have stirred the same controversy among both Northerners and Southerners. The fact that Lincoln, as president of a divided union, wrote the document is most important because only he enjoyed the authority, under the chief executive's war powers, to do so. *Where* the Emancipation Proclamation was insignificant.

On the other hand, the Germantown Protest of 1688 could have been written only in the Philadelphia area because of the inextricable relationship of the city's early Quaker population to that document. The Germantown Protest reflects the budding abolitionist convictions that eventually prevailed among Philadelphia's Quakers because of their religious beliefs in the equality of all human beings. Nowhere else in the colonies at that time and among no other group of people could the document have been written.

Why? Why did the author write the document? The question of motive is the most difficult one to answer. In an edited collection of documents, there is frequently an explanation of motive preceding the document. However, for original works if teachers provide students with some background information as well as some information about the author, they will have the necessary historical context to make an educated guess as to the author's motive.

So What? This is another way of asking, Why is the document important in the broader context of American history, and in this case, what is its importance to the institutions of slavery and/or the Underground Railroad? If the document is not significant, it should probably not be used in the course. In responding to this question, students should consider the purpose of the document, what it reveals about the author's opinion or bias, and the conclusions they can draw from it.

The documents in this section are reprinted as they were written, without editorial changes or grammatical corrections. These sources were interpreted by middle school students using the six questions identified previously. Each document is followed by one or more student interpretations and a teacher's assessment of those interpretations. The quality of the critical thinking and writing differs among the various student samples, but collectively the samples will give teachers a better understanding of how they can apply document analyses in their own classes, offer insight into grading those analyses, and give an idea of what to expect from students.

Analyzing Contemporary Documents

Public Declarations

Antislavery declarations described the operating principles and beliefs of the abolitionists who drafted them. Many of these documents were created at local, state, or national antislavery conventions in order to summarize the points of agreement that were reached at the gatherings. Other documents came in the form of a protest against slavery and detailed the reasons for a group's opposition to the institution. Still others were legal documents, defining the federal government's policies with regard to the institution of slavery. Two of the most famous antislavery documents are the Germantown Protest of 1688 and President Abraham Lincoln's Emancipation Proclamation, which was issued on September 22, 1862, and went into effect on January 1, 1863. Taken together, the two documents mark the beginnings and end of the struggle to abolish slavery in the United States.

THE GERMANTOWN PROTEST, 1688

This is to ye monthly meeting held at Richard Worrell's.

These are the reasons why we are against the traffick of men-body, as followeth. Is there any that would be done or handled in this manner? viz., to be sold or made a slave for all the time of his life? How fearful and faint-hearted are many at see [sic] when they see a strange vessel—being afraid it should be a Turk, and they should be taken, and sold for slaves into Turkey. Now what is this better done, as Turks do? Yea, rather it is worse for them which say they are Christians, for we hear that ye most part of such negars are brought hitherto against their will and consent and that many of them are stolen. Now tho they are black we cannot conceive there is more liberty to have them slaves, as it is to have other white ones. There is a saying that we shall do to all men like as we will be done ourselves; making no difference of what generation, descent or colour they are. And those who steal or rob men, and those who buy or purchase them, are they not alike? Here is liberty of conscience which is right and reasonable; here ought to be likewise liberty of ye body, except evil-doers, which is another case. But to bring men hither, or to rob and sell them against their will, we stand against. In Europe there are many oppressed for conscience sake; and here are those opposed which are of a black colour. And we who know that all men must not commit adultery—some do commit adultery, in others, separating wives from their husbands and giving them to others; and some sell the children of these poor creatures to other men. Ah! do consider well this thing, you who do it, if you would be done of this manner? And if it is done according to Christianity? You surpass Holland and Germany in this thing. This makes an ill report in all those countries of Europe, where they hear off, that ye Quakers do here handle men as they handle their cattle. And for that reason some have no mind or inclination to come hither. And who shall maintain this your course, or plead for it? Truly we cannot do so, except you shall inform us better hereof, viz., that Christians have liberty to practice these things. Pray, what thing in the world can be done worse towards us, than if men should rob or steal us away, and sell us for slaves to strange countries; separating husbands from their wives and children. Being now this is not done in the manner we would be done at thereof we contradict and are against this traffic of men-body. And we who profess that it is not lawful to steal, must, likewise, avoid to purchase such things as are stolen, but rather help to stop this robbing and stealing if possible. And such men ought to be delivered out of ye hands of ye robbers, and set free as well as in Europe. Then is Pennsylvania to have a good report, instead it hath now a bad one for this sake in other countries. Especially whereas ye Europeans are desirous to know in what manner ye Quakers do rule in their province—and most of them do look upon us with an envious eye. But if this is done well, what shall we say is done evil?

If once these slaves (which they say are so wicked and stubborn men) should join themselves—fight for their freedom—and handle their masters and mistresses as they did handle them before; will these masters and mistresses take the sword of hand and war against these poor slaves, like we are able to believe, some will not refuse to do; or have these negars not as much right to fight for their freedom, as you have to keep them slaves?

Now consider well this thing, if it is good or bad? And in case you find it to be good to handle these blacks at that manner, we desire and require you hereby lovingly that you may inform us herein, which at this time never was done, viz. that Christians have such a liberty to do so. To the end we shall be satisfied in this point, and satisfy likewise our good friends and acquaintances in our native country, to whose it is a terror, or fearful thing that men should be handled in Pennsylvania.

This is from our meeting at Germantown, held ye 18 of the 2 month, 1688, to be delivered to the Monthly Meeting at Richard Worrell's.

Garret Hendricks
Derick up de Graeff
Francis Daniel Pastorius
Abraham up Den Graef

For those students who have difficulty translating the document, the following is an abbreviated version of the text with more modern spelling and punctuation:

> These are the reasons why we are against slavery: Is there anyone that would want be handled in this manner? To be sold or made a slave for his entire life? How fearful are sailors on the sea when they see a strange ship, being afraid that it is piloted by Turks and that they will be captured and sold as slaves in Turkey? Now is slave trading any better than what the Turks do? It is worse for those who say they are Christians when they bring Africans to America against their will. Many of these Africans are stolen.
>
> Although they are black, we do not believe that they should be slaves anymore than white people should be slaves. There is a saying that we shall do to all men, like as we will be done to ourselves; making no difference of what generation, descent, or color they are. And those who steal or rob men and those who buy or purchase them, are they not all alike? Here in Pennsylvania we believe in the liberty of conscience, which is right and reasonable. Shouldn't we also enjoy the liberty of the body, except for those who break the law? And yet there are those men who force black slaves to commit adultery by separating wives from their husbands and giving them to others, and some sell the children of those poor creatures to other men. Oh, do consider well these things and if it is done according to Christianity? We are against this traffic in men's bodies. And we who believe that it is not lawful to steal, must also avoid purchasing those things that are stolen, but rather help to stop this robbing and stealing. Black men should be delivered out of the hands of the robbers and set free here as well as in Europe. Only then will Pennsylvania have a good report.
>
> If once these slaves (which they say are wicked and stubborn) should join themselves together and fight for their freedom and handle their masters and mistresses as slaves; will these masters and mistresses take the sword at hand and war against these poor slaves? Or have these Negroes not as much right to fight for their freedom as you have to keep them slaves?

The Germantown Protest of 1688 was written by four German-speaking Quakers—Garret Hendricks, Derick op de Graeff, Francis Daniell Pastorius, and Abraham op den Graef—and became known to history as the first anti-slavery petition in America. The petition was submitted to the Philadelphia Yearly Meeting, the governing body of Friends in the Middle Atlantic states, but no action was taken. Not until 1776 did the Yearly Meeting make slave-holding a cause for disownment in the Society of Friends.

STUDENT INTERPRETATION 1

1. *What kind of document is this? What is the document about?*
   This is a protest against slavery. It is a speech.

2. *Who wrote the document?*

   Age: 30 to 50   *Sex:* male   *Occupation:* Unknown

   Married/Unmarried: married   *Children:* unknown

   Residence: Germantown, PA   *Able to Write:* yes, but poor spelling

   Other Information: the writers are Quakers

3. *When was the document written?* February 18, 1688

4. *Where was the document written?* In Germantown, outside of Philadelphia

5. *Why was the document written?* To end slavery with Quakers. Writers hate slavery.

6. *What is the significance of the document?* It shows how Quaker beliefs are in conflict with slavery.

This student chose to provide only the most basic responses to the questions given on the Document Analysis sheet. This is a common approach for middle school students, especially if they are just being introduced to the exercise of interpreting a primary source document. While the analysis is lacking in abstract thinking, there are some important observations. First, the student identifies the fact that the document is a "protest against slavery" and realizes that it is a *public* pronouncement, though he refers to it as a speech. Second, the student identifies the age range of the authors as thirty to fifty years old, though there is no direct reference to their ages in the document. The assumption here is that a document of this importance was composed by men of advanced age and experience. Similarly, the documentary references to the act of slave traders "separating wives from their husbands and giving them to others" probably led the student to believe that the authors could sympathize with the plight of the slaves because they, too, were married. Third, the student recognizes the difference between contemporary and seventeenth-century spelling of words like *traffick* and *colour*. Finally, there is the important recognition that the document was written by Quakers and that the beliefs of Friends are somehow inconsistent with the practice of slavery. All of these observations are critical to interpreting the document and, as such, are important starting points. But this student will need more guidance in understanding the significance of the protest.

Here's a better-developed interpretation of the same document.

STUDENT INTERPRETATION 2

In 1688, when this Germantown Protest was written, slavery was up and coming in the United States. There were slaves in both the North and South. But there were some people in the North who protested against slavery. Garret Hendricks, Derrick Up de Graeff, Francis Daniell Pastorius and Abraham Up den Graef were some of these people.

"It is worse for those who say they are Christians when they bring Africans to America against their will." Slavery needed to be stopped.

This document is a formal document protesting slavery. "Although they are black, we do not believe that they should be slaves any more than white people should be slaves." "It is worse for those who say they are Christians when they bring Africans to America against their will." These are reasons why this document tried to abolish slavery.

The people who wrote this document were males in their early to mid thirties, who were most likely community leaders. They lived in Germantown, PA. They were probably married and had children. They were educated and able to write.

Unfortunately, the document had no effect on slavery because it continued in the United States until 1865.

Unlike the first student interpretation, this one is written in essay form and reflects more advanced abstract thinking and writing skills. The student makes an important distinction between the South, where slavery went unchallenged, and the North, where there were those "who protested against slavery" as early as 1688. He also explains that the protest "had no effect on slavery because it continued in the United States until 1865."

To be sure, middle schoolers tend to think in absolute terms. It is difficult for them to understand that the protest against slavery was a *gradual* process that was just beginning in 1688. Like other social justice movements, abolitionism began with a small group of individuals who identified the injustice and appealed to a larger body of people to address the problem. In this case, Hendricks, Pastorius, and the Up de Graeffs represent that small but socially conscious group. Their appeal was addressed to members of their church, the Religious Society of Friends, or Quakers. While Quakers, as a body, did not adopt abolitionism as a formal policy until 1776, historians have credited the Germantown Protest with inspiring the beginnings of the abolitionist cause among Friends. Of course, the student would need to have more background information to make this kind of connection.

Interestingly, while the student does cite the group's Christian beliefs as "reasons why this document tried to abolish slavery," the fact that they are Quakers escapes him. One might expect that a student with strong abstract thinking skills would recognize the several references to Quakers and Monthly Meeting in the document as an indication that these particular Christians were members of the Society of Friends. However, the inconsistency is typical for this age group.

At the same time, the interpretation reflects an advanced ability to use direct quotation as evidence to support the student's point of view. The integration of primary source quotation into a student's interpretation is a fundamental skill in the writing of history at the higher levels of education because it demonstrates the student's ability to understand the document as well as how the document supports his own argument. This skill should be introduced at the middle school level. As the student goes on to high school he will learn how to fragment the quotation and integrate only the most important parts of the quotation with his own explanation, rather than insert full-sentence quotations as this student does. Still, the fact that he attempts this skill is impressive.

A much better-known document is the Emancipation Proclamation, issued by President Abraham Lincoln on September 22, 1862. This executive order freed the slaves in the states controlled by the Confederate government only and went into effect on January 1, 1863. As students read through the document, they should be asked to consider four questions: (1) Why didn't Lincoln free the slaves in the border states? (2) Why did he distinguish certain parts of the Southern states in rebellion? (3) Did Lincoln actually have the authority to free slaves in the territories controlled by the Confederacy? and (4) Why had he changed his mind in September 1862 to tie emancipation to his original war aim of preserving the union?

THE EMANCIPATION PROCLAMATION

Whereas, on the twenty-second day of September, in the year of our Lord one thousand eight hundred and sixty-two, a proclamation was issued by the President of the United States, containing, among other things, the following, to wit:

That on the first day of January, in the year of our Lord one thousand eight hundred and sixty-three, all persons held as slaves within any State, or designated part of a State, the people whereof shall then be in rebellion against the United States, shall be then, thenceforward, and forever free; and the Executive Government of the United States, including the military and naval authority thereof, will recognize and maintain the freedom of such persons, and will do no act or acts to repress such persons, or any of them, in any efforts they may make for their actual freedom.

That the Executive will, on the first day of January aforesaid, by proclamation, designate the States and parts of States, if any, in which the people thereof respectively shall then be in rebellion against the United States; and the fact that any State, or the people thereof, shall on that day be in good faith represented in the Congress of the United States by members chosen thereunto at elections wherein a majority of the qualified voters of such State shall have participated, shall in the absence of strong countervailing testimony be deemed conclusive evidence that such State and the people thereof are not then in rebellion against the United States.

Now, therefore, I, Abraham Lincoln, President of the United States, by virtue of the power in me vested as Commander-in-Chief of the Army and Navy of the United States, in time of actual armed rebellion against the authority and government of the United States, and in a fit and necessary war measure for suppressing said rebellion, do on this first day of January, in the year of our Lord one thousand eight hundred and sixty-three, and in accordance with my purpose so to do, publicly proclaimed for the full period of 100 days from the day first above mentioned, order and designate as the States and parts of States wherein the people thereof, respectively, are this day in rebellion against the United States, the following, to wit:

Arkansas, Texas, Louisiana (except the parishes of St. Bernard, Plaquemines, Jefferson, St. John, St. Charles, St. James, Ascension, Assumption, Terre Bonne, Lafourche, St. Mary, St. Martin, and Orleans, including the city of New Orleans), Mississippi, Alabama, Florida, Georgia, South Carolina, North Carolina, and Virginia (except the forty-eight counties designated as West Virginia, and also the counties of Berkeley, Accomac, Northampton, Elizabeth City, York, Princess Anne, and Norfolk, including the cities of Norfolk and Portsmouth) and which excepted parts are for the present left precisely as if this proclamation were not issued.

And by virtue of the power and for the purpose aforesaid, I do order and declare that all persons held as slaves within said designated States and parts of States are, and henceforward shall be, free; and that the Executive Government of the United States, including the military and naval authorities thereof, shall recognize and maintain the freedom of said persons.

And I hereby enjoin upon the people so declared to be free to abstain from all violence, unless in necessary self-defense; and I recommend to them that, in all cases where allowed, they labor faithfully for reasonable wages.

And I further declare and make known that such persons of suitable condition will be received into the armed service of the United States to garrison forts, positions, stations, and other places, and to man vessels of all sorts in said service.

And upon this act, sincerely believed to be an act of justice, warranted by the Constitution upon military necessity, I invoke the considerate judgment of mankind and the gracious favor of Almighty God.

In witness whereof, I have hereunto set my hand and caused the seal of the United States to be affixed.

Done at the city of Washington, the first day of January, in the year of our Lord one thousand eight hundred and sixty-three, and of the independence of the United States of America the eighty-seventh.

By the President: Abraham Lincoln
William H. Seward, Secretary of State

STUDENT INTERPRETATION

The document is called the *Emancipation Proclamation*. It was issued by President Abraham Lincoln in 1862. But the proclamation would not be made a law until January 1, 1863.

The document says that all "persons held as slaves within any State, or designated part of a State in rebellion against the United States will be set forever free." This proclamation applied to slaves in the <u>South</u>, but excluded the 48 counties that represented West Virginia and also the Virginia counties of Berkeley, Accomac, Northampton, Elizabeth City, York, Princess Anne and Norfolk. The proclamation does not apply to the border states because they remained loyal to the North. That sounds like a contradiction but it was important to keep those states on the North's side in the Civil War.

The author of the document is President Abraham Lincoln. He was a member of the Republican Party and believed that slavery was wrong. He was able to pass this proclamation because of his authority as the leader of the United States Army. The fourth paragraph shows this authority saying that "I, Abraham Lincoln, President of the United States, by virtue of the power in me vested as Commander-in-Chief of the Army and Navy of the United States, in time of actual armed rebellion." He called this proclamation a "war measure."

By writing the *Emancipation Proclamation*, Lincoln made slavery an issue in the Civil War. By 1862 he realized that ending slavery was just as important as preserving the Union. He understood his responsibility as the President to protect the well being of this country and everyone in it.

This student demonstrates a nice balance of concrete and abstract thinking. His careful reading of the document allows him to avoid the common mistake made by other middle schoolers who believe that the Emancipation Proclamation freed *all* the slaves, both in the South and in the border states. That result was actually achieved by the passage of the Thirteenth Amendment to the United States Constitution in 1865. Instead the student makes two important distinctions: (1) that the proclamation applied only to the *South* (even underlining the word) and (2) that there were specific areas of the South—some Virginia counties and the state of West Virginia—that were also exempt.

Just as insightful is the student's remark that the failure to free slaves in the border states "sounds like a contradiction" if Lincoln actually believed that slavery was morally wrong. At the same time, the student seems to recognize that Lincoln acted in a politically expedient fashion by allowing slavery in those states in order to keep them in the Union and fighting on for the North.

But the issue of Lincoln's motive for drafting the proclamation needed to be more fully developed, especially given this student's appreciation for the political reasons for limiting emancipation. While the student's insight that "Lincoln made slavery an issue in the Civil War" by issuing the Emancipation Proclamation explains the president's belief that, by 1862, "ending slavery was just as important as preserving the Union," he does not take into consideration the host of factors that figured into the president's decision. To do this, a teacher may want to suggest the issue of motive to the student. Why, for example, did Lincoln decide to free the slaves in 1863 instead of from the very start of his presidential administration in 1861? Was it a decision based on political considerations? Did his religious beliefs influence the decision? Students might consider what influences shape their own decision-making processes or those of the current president. Teachers may also suggest that the student consult some outside readings or a website on Lincoln to better understand his decision.

In fact, Lincoln issued the Emancipation Proclamation in part to quiet his abolitionist critics, who charged that his reluctance to declare slaves free was prolonging the Civil War, and partly in pursuit of his abolitionist convictions and original war aim to preserve the union. Hoping that an emancipation policy would not be interpreted as the act of a desperate administration to raise a servile insurrection, Lincoln waited for a Union victory before issuing the proclamation. The Battle of Antietam, fought on September 17, 1862, provided him with that victory.[1] Still, the quality of explanation in this essay as well as the skill with which the student integrates primary source quotation with his own explanation of the document is the type of work one might expect from a high school junior.

Fugitive Slave Advertisements

Fugitive slave advertisements present a rare view into the slave culture of antebellum America as well as into the lives of the runaways themselves. Advertisements were designed to identify as precisely as possible information about men and women who left behind few other personal records. Often these published notices contained information about their physical characteristics—age, height, sex, skin color, scars and bodily markings—as well as the type of clothing they wore. Some notices offer clues about the daily life of the slaves, including the type of work they performed, marriage status, frequency of escapes, and connections to family and friends. Additionally, the advertisements offer the subjective assessments of the owners, who tended to classify runaways with such terms as *cunning, impudent, bold,* and *complacent,* among others.

The following fugitive slave advertisement was taken from the November 29, 1809, edition of the *Chester and Delaware Federalist:*

TAKE NOTICE.

WAS taken up, on suspicion of being a run-away, and now confined in the gaol of Chester county, Pennsylvania, a

Black Man,

who calls himself, SHADRACK MACKLIN, appears to be about 21 or 22 years of age; about 5 feet 7 or 8 inches high; full face; thick lips; and small scar under his right eye; says he was brought up with Sampson Davis, a colored man and house carpenter, near Milford, Sussex county, state of Delaware and set free by him, March 1809, but has no credentials to show this was the case.

Any person owning said black man, is desired to come forward, prove his property, pay charges and take him away before the 17th of December next, otherwise he will be discharged from prison.

THOMAS EVANS

West Chester, PA Nov. 15, 1809

STUDENT INTERPRETATION

Document title: Newspaper article from the <u>Chester and Delaware Federalist,</u> November 29, 1809.

What kind of document is this? The document is like a 19th century version of our lost and found notices for missing children and pets. The document tells the reader that a slave by the name of Shadrick Macklin has been found and needs to be claimed or he will be set free. The articles briefly describes Mr. Macklin then tells how he should be claimed.

Who wrote the document? Thomas Evans

What other characteristics can you tell about the runaway?
Age: 21 or 22 years old   *Sex:* Male   *Race:* Black
Height: 5 feet, 7 or 8 inches
Also has full face, thick lips and a small scar under his right eye
When was the document written? The document was written on November 15, 1809, but wasn't printed by the newspaper until 14 days later, on November 29, 1809.

Where was the document written? West Chester, Pennsylvania

Why was the document written? The document was written to try to help a slave owner claim his slave. It was written for the general public and for readers of the <u>Chester and Delaware Federalist</u>. Basically, this document was written to inform all the newspaper's readers in the states of Pennsylvania and Delaware.

What is the significance of the document? This article tells me how slaves would be claimed in the 1800s and that slavery was still supported in Pennsylvania in 1809, even though it was abolished in the state in 1780.

The student offers a detailed description of the advertisement as well as two important insights. First, she notes that the advertisement is "like a 19th century version of our lost and found notices for missing children and pets." This is a wonderful connection to make between the nineteenth and twenty-first centuries, especially since the teacher can build on it to describe the legal status of a slave as the property of his white master. The implication here is that the slave, like a pet, was treated as "property" rather than as a human being. The student also notes the reference to "thick lips," "black" complexion, and "small scar under his right eye," which emphasizes the fugitive's bodily condition and reinforces his value as property. If the student can make this type of connection, teachers will be able to build on that knowledge by explaining that such references serve as important descriptors and also reflect the common profile of the earliest runaways as having a dark complexion. Advertisements indicate that 70 percent of the runaways during the period 1790 to 1816 were so dark-skinned that they were described as "black" and possessed strong Negroid features such as "thick lips."[2]

Second, the student writes that the significance of the advertisement lies in the fact that "slavery was still supported in Pennsylvania in 1809, even though it was abolished in the state in 1780." Although I wish she had developed that thought a bit more, the acknowledgment of that fact demonstrates some important background knowledge. Teachers may want to use these fugitive slave advertisements to introduce a unit on slavery and/or abolitionism and elicit some critical questions around which to organize the unit, such as: What kinds of slaves decided to run away and why? How do fugitive slave advertisements help us understand the legal status of a slave in antebellum America? and Why did a Pennsylvania newspaper run slave advertisements in 1809 when that state had abolished slavery in 1780? This particular advertisement is especially useful for answering the first question about the kinds of slaves who ran away.

Shadrack Macklin was, like most slaves who attempted escape during the early years of the Underground Railroad, a single young man in his early twenties. Advertisements from Virginia, Tennessee, Louisiana, and the Carolinas dating to the period 1790 to 1816 reveal that males in their late teens and twenties composed 81 percent of the runaways and 78 percent of them were between the ages of thirteen and twenty-nine.[3] Single, young men ran away because they did not have the responsibilities of a family and they were more willing than females to challenge the authority of masters and overseers. Once they set out on the route to freedom, young male runaways were better able to defend themselves and resist capture.[4] Young slave women, on the other hand, were less likely to run away because of child-rearing responsibilities. Even if they did not have their own children to care for, slave women in their teens and early twenties were expected to care for other children in the slave community and, in some cases, the master's children as well. This did not mean that they were any less desirous of freedom than their male counterparts, but rather that they understood that carrying children in flight to the North would slow their passage and make them more vulnerable to capture.[5] This pattern changed after the 1820s, when female slaves escaped in increasing numbers, sometimes with their children in tow, especially after the passage of the Fugitive Slave Act of 1850. The following advertisement from the October 6, 1857, edition of the *Charlestown [South Carolina] Mercury* reflects these changing circumstances:

$500 REWARD. —RANAWAY

about three years ago, a mulatto girly named CEELY, rather short and thickset, about 28 or 30 years of age, light complexion; has a small scar on her upper lip, near the mouth; her upper teeth bad, near gums; a fine seamstress, mantua maker and tailoress; has often been seen about the city since she went off, and is supposed to be harbored (as she has been heretofore) by some white person. Five hundred dollars will be paid for her apprehension, and fifty dollars on proof to conviction of any responsible person who may have harbored her.

WM. R. TABER.

Charlestown, SC October 6, 1857

STUDENT INTERPRETATION

The kind of document I decided to do my essay on was a newspaper article. It describes the features of a female runaway slave named Ceely. She was a seamstress about 28 or 30 years of age. She escaped from her master in 1854, three years before the article was written.

A quote that I thought was important was "Five Hundred dollars will be paid for her apprehension, and fifty dollars on proof to conviction of any responsible person who may have harbored her." After reading this quote, you can see that most slaves were treated as trash and not as real humans.

Knowing who wrote the article is also important. In this article, William Taber was the author. He was a slave owner who might have been a leader in his community of Charlestown, South Carolina. I say this because he seems to be wealthy. Anyone offering to pay $550 for the return of a runaway slave must have been wealthy because that was a lot of money back then. My guess is that Taber wanted Ceely back because she was one of the best slaves he owned. She might have even been a house servant because slaves with lighter skin were thought to be better than those who were darker skinned and worked in the fields.

This document is important because it shows how different black slaves were treated from white people. The description of Ceely's skin color, teeth, and short thick body is insulting. It's like she was an animal or a piece of property.

This student demonstrates some good inductive reasoning. She notes that William Taber, the slaveholder, was most likely wealthy because he is "offering to pay $550 for the return of [his] slave." She also states that his emphasis on describing the runaway's physical characteristics leads the student to believe that Ceely was treated like "an animal or a piece of property." More insightful is the student's recognition of social status based on skin color. She points out that Taber offers such a high reward for Ceely because she "might have . . . been a house servant." The student clarifies the point by explaining that "slaves with lighter skin were thought to be better than those who were darker skinned and worked in the fields." This is an exceptional insight for a middle school student to make as it reflects the kind of higher-order thinking more often associated with high school. Not all students will recognize this subtlety.

Teachers might encourage students to think about the social hierarchy that was prevalent in antebellum America—among both blacks and whites—by having them consider the historic connotations of color in our society. Ask students, for example, what adjectives come to mind when they think about the color white. Many will probably mention *purity, goodness,* and *cleanliness.* What about the color black? Some may respond with such words as *darkness, dirty, evil.* It was no different in antebellum society, when white people were generally treated as if they belonged to a higher social class than people of color. Even within the African American race, those slaves with lighter complexions were often favored by their masters and used as house servants. Of course, teachers must make clear to students that while these connotations are not an acceptable way to treat any human being, regardless of her skin color, it was an acceptable method of defining a person during the nineteenth century.

Ceely, the "mulatto," or a person of mixed racial ancestry, the focus of the previous advertisement, may very well have been a house servant because of her light complexion. To be sure, mulattoes escaped in increasingly greater numbers after the 1820s, with as much as a 43 percent increase by 1860. Light-skinned slaves enjoyed certain advantages if they decided to escape. Not only were they were more likely to pass for white people, but their skills could also allow them to find employment in free society more readily than fugitives of a darker hue because they often held positions as house servants, maids, cooks, and barbers on the slave plantation. Mulattoes were also twice as likely to be literate as black fugitives. They often carried freedom papers or passes forged by their own hand and could assimilate more easily into the free black population of a major Northern city.[6]

Antebellum Diaries and Journals

Diaries and journals offer some unique insight into the operation of, routes on, and participants in the Underground Railroad. Students and teachers can easily access these sources on the Web at the sites listed in the annotated bibliography. Quakers, in particular, were known for recording their daily activities as a way of reflecting on their spiritual lives. Farmers also kept diaries as a way of recording seasonal change and weather patterns that might have an impact on their planting or harvest. Often, their political views, family history, and social goings-on found their way into these accounts as well.

David Evans (1818–1898), a Quaker farmer and schoolteacher from Willistown, Chester County, Pennsylvania, kept such a diary. He was the son of Nathan Evans, an outspoken Quaker minister whose antislavery messages were not always appreciated by his more conservative neighbors as well as the members of Willistown Friends Meeting, where the family worshipped. While Nathan was eventually disowned from the Willistown Meeting because of his illegal involvement in the Underground Railroad, David was more secretive about his abolitionist beliefs as well as his own involvement with the

Underground Railroad. However, his two-volume journal in the collections of the Chester County Historical Society offers special insight into his clandestine activities.

Students may be introduced to the diary through the following 1836 entry, which describes an antislavery meeting at the Willistown Friends School House and establishes the important connection between abolitionist efforts in a local community and the larger statewide movement in Pennsylvania:

> 8 mo.–12–1836: Fifth day evening last, the first meeting on the subject of Anti-Slavery which has been held in this neighborhood took place last evening at our school house. It was well attended and a great interest manifested by the audience. William Whitehead from West Chester gave us a very pertinent and manly address. The call for a state convention and the declaration of principles published by a meeting at Adelphia Hall in Philadelphia was read. A committee was appointed to bring forward the names of delegates to attend the State convention and made report to a meeting to be held at the same place on the first 7th day of next year. The meeting terminated without disturbance and was altogether calculated to leave a favorable impression.

Note the references to the calling of a state convention and the committee "appointed to bring forward the names of delegates to attend the State convention" at this local antislavery gathering. Both of these references underscore the grassroots nature of the antislavery movement. Like the Religious Society of Friends, whose members condemned the institution of slavery on spiritual and moral grounds, the antislavery movement had a hierarchical organization. Operational principles and policies were drafted at state conventions by delegates who represented smaller, regional antislavery societies. The delegates were the most respected and active members of the local societies.

Another point to register with students is that the Quakers had a custom of referring to months and days by numbers to avoid giving homage to the pagan gods for whom some were named. This practice was consistent with the Quaker belief in a simple or plain lifestyle, which emphasized practical behavior and specifically the avoidance of any extravagance in dress, personal behavior, language, or vocabulary.[7] Thus, Sunday was called First Day, Monday, Second Day, and so on. January was the First Month, February, the Second Month, and so on. In the previous entry, "8 mo." refers to August, and "Fifth day" refers to Thursday.

The following excerpts are taken from the year 1842. Evans was a twenty-four-year-old schoolteacher at the time he wrote these entries. He also provides the reader with some keen insight into the operation of the local Underground Railroad station and how he conducted business at his station:

> Fifth day morning last, I started about 2 A.M. and took 4 colored persons to the Anti-Slavery office in Philadelphia. They were sent on by J. Fulton the evening before in care of Henry Lee, a colored man. Two more weary travelers from the land of bondage came last evening on their way to Canada.

> Fifth day morning about 2 o'clock Lukens Pierce drove up in a farm wagon containing 27 colored persons—13 adults and 14 children. Fifth day evening I took 13 of them—5 women, 3 men and 5 children to the Anti-Slavery office in Philadelphia in E. Passmore's dearborn [covered wagon] and with his horses. Last night Davis Garrett, Jr., and John Wright, a colored young man took the rest of them down in two dearborns.

> An anti-slavery meeting was held in Joseph Hickman's house fifth day p.m. Another was held in our schoolhouse in the evening. Dr. Irwin lectured. I attended the one in the afternoon. Lucretia Mott and F. Douglass, a runaway were also there, but he left early fearing that he might be arrested.

> On fourth day night Henry Lee took 5 colored people to town—two women and 3 children. On Sixth day night Father took 16 more, all men. This company of men came from Harrisburg and would not have disgraced any Station so far as we may judge from their behavior while here. We had supper prepared for them in the evening so that all might sit down together. As I observed their conduct toward each other at the table, I thought that they were much above the generality of whites among us in point of breeding.

STUDENT INTERPRETATION 1

David Evans was a white Quaker man who believed in antislavery. He was also a father, husband, schoolteacher and had a variety of other jobs. He kept a diary that kept records about what went on at his underground railroad station. It also tells about how he helped many slaves escape during the night or very early in the morning hours: "Fifth day morning about 2 o'clock Lukens Pierce drove up in a farm wagon containing 27 colored persons."

David Evans was an 80 year-old man when he died. He started writing this diary when he was about 17 years old. He was married and had children. He was the founder of the borough of Malvern. David Evans was also a minister.

He wrote this diary sometime between 1835 and 1898. During this time period there was a lot of slavery going on. There were also a lot of slaves escaping North. He wrote the diary to keep track of how many black and white people helped and to remember what went on in his meetings. He may have also written it so that other people could read it to know what went on. The document is important because it lets people know what was happening to slaves and that there were some good people who tried to do something to end it.

Although this essay might appear to be strictly descriptive in nature, it does contain some important points about the operation of the Underground Railroad. First, the student identifies the fact that the agents Evans worked with conducted fugitives between stations at night to escape notice by the authorities. Second, she identifies the interracial nature of the secret route to freedom, noting that Evans kept the diary "to keep track of how many black and white people helped." Blacks like Henry Lee and John Wright served as conductors. Whites like J. Fulton, E. Passmore, Lucretia Mott, and Evans himself were stationmasters. Whether or not the student fully understands the implications of these two patterns is another matter. But at least it's a starting point for her teacher to develop as the class continues its study of the Underground Railroad.

The following student offers a more developed—and creative—analysis of the Evans diary entries:

STUDENT INTERPRETATION 2

David Evans closed his diary and walked to the door, someone was knocking. He answered the door and discovered "two more weary travelers from the land of bondage who were on their way to Canada." He quickly welcomed them inside his house, making sure that no one saw his illegal actions.

The scene happened 160 years ago and was written down by David Evans in the journal he kept since he was a little boy. Evans had a negative outlook on slavery from an early age because his parents were "ardent abolitionists and station masters on the Underground Railroad." He also thought that the runaways were smarter than the white people he knew because when he "observed their conduct toward each other at the table, I thought that they were much above the generality of whites among us in point of breeding."

In 1842 when these diary entries were made, Evans was 24 years old. He probably wanted to keep a record of runaway slaves to know how many of them he helped and what happened to them if their families came looking for them.

The Underground Railroad was an illegal movement because of the Fugitive Slave Law. If Evans was caught or his diary was found by a slave owner or a government official, he would have been arrested and sent to jail. Today his diary is important because historians and researchers can get a good idea of how the Underground Railroad operated.

This student not only uses primary source quotes to support her argument but explains some key insights into the risks an abolitionist took when he decided to participate on the Underground Railroad. Her contention that Evans "would have been arrested and sent to jail" if "his diary was found by a slave owner or a government official" is an illustration of this point. Additionally, Evans would have incriminated all those agents he named in the diary. Another good insight is provided in the student's remark that Evans "had a negative outlook on slavery from an early age because his parents were 'ardent abolitionists and station masters on the Underground Railroad.'" Among all the white agents, Quakers, in particular, sympathized with the plight of the slaves because of their religious conviction in the spiritual equality of all human beings. Accordingly, those Friends who became active on the Underground Railroad usually inculcated the same beliefs in their children. Predictably, for the Evans family, involvement in this illegal movement was a family affair.

Finally, the student offers a fascinating insight into Evans' perception of the slaves, who were generally considered intellectually inferior. She writes that the Quaker schoolteacher "thought runaways were smarter than the white people he knew" and then supports the point with Evans' own observation that "their conduct toward each other at the table" was "much above the generality of whites among us in point of breeding." The reference is similar to William Still's finding that runaways were "in general, more intelligent than most slaves" and helps to dispel the myth that runaways were intellectually inferior and passive recipients in the movement.[8]

Letters

Letters were more common among Underground Railroad agents than diaries and journals, probably because they served the more practical purpose of conveying information that was needed immediately. In addition, most letters were destroyed once they were read to avoid the possibility of incrimination.

William Still, a free black abolitionist who coordinated the Eastern Line of the Underground Railroad from the offices of the Pennsylvania Antislavery Society in Philadelphia, was perhaps the most prodigious letter writer. He also had a sense of history and preserved his correspondence, hiding it in a local cemetery until after the passage of the Thirteenth Amendment outlawed slavery in the United States.[9] In 1872 Still used the correspondence to write and publish an eight-hundred-page book titled *The Underground Railroad*. Not only does the book provide a rare eyewitness account, but it is also considered by historians to be the most accurate source ever written on the secret passage to freedom. The following letter is taken from Still's book.[10]

Wilmington, 12th Mo. 1st, 1860

RESPECTED FRIEND, WILLIAM STILL: —I write to let thee know that Harriet Tubman is again in these parts. She arrived last evening from one of the trips of mercy to God's poor, bringing two men with her as far as New Castle. I agreed to pay a man last evening to pilot them on their way to Chester County. The wife of one of the men, with two or three children, was left some thirty miles below, and I gave Harriet ten dollars to hire a man with carriage to take them to Chester County. She said a man had offered for that sum, to bring them on. I shall be very uneasy about them, until I hear they are safe. There is now much more risk on the road, than there has been for several months past, as we find that some poor worthless wretches are constantly on the look out on two roads, that they cannot well avoid, especially with carriage; yet as it is Harriet, who seemed to have had a special agent to guard her on her journey of mercy, I have hope.

Thy friend,
Thomas Garrett

STUDENT INTERPRETATION

William Still is sometimes called the "Father of the Underground Railroad." He was a famous abolitionist who tried to help free slaves and help them escape to freedom. He received this particular letter from Thomas Garrett concerning Harriet Tubman's whereabouts. Garrett informed Still that Harriet was in "their parts" and that her journey would be dangerous and unsafe. In the letter he states, "I gave Harriet $10 to hire a man with carriage to take them to Chester County." He also told Still that she had a "special agent" with her to help lead the way.

Thomas Garrett is the author of the letter. He was also a station master on the Underground Railroad, just like Still was. Garrett is a male in his 30s or 40s. He resides in Wilmington, Delaware, an active part of the Underground Railroad where a lot of "safe houses" and abolitionists were located.

This document was written on December 1, 1860. During this time, the Underground Railroad was most likely at its highest peak, probably because slaves passed word of freedom in the North through songs, quilts and stories.

Garrett wrote the letter because he wanted Still to know where Harriet Tubman was and that he was very concerned about her safety. The letter shows how the Underground Railroad operated between Wilmington, Delaware, where Garrett lived, and Philadelphia, where Still lived. It also shows that both of these men were good friends who put their lives at risk to help runaway slaves.

This student demonstrates a strong ability to integrate fact, concept and explanation in her writing. She opens with the concept "William Still is sometimes called the 'Father of the Underground Railroad'" and explains why in the next sentence. The student tells us that Still was "a famous abolitionist who tried to help free slaves and help them escape to freedom" and also reinforces his critical role by revealing his association with two other famous agents, Thomas Garrett and Harriet Tubman. In this sense, the essay does a nice job of describing the content of the letter as well as offering the student's insight into its importance.

The interpretation also demonstrates some good deductive reasoning in the third and fourth paragraphs. After the student identifies the date of the letter as December 1, 1860, she places it in a historical context by noting that "the Underground Railroad was most likely at its highest peak" at this time. She then surmises that the popularity of the movement was "probably because slaves passed word of freedom in the North through songs, quilts and stories." Whether conscious or not, her wording demonstrates intellectual honesty. To be sure, there was greater accessibility to the Underground Railroad for all the reasons she mentions by 1860. But the mythology of the movement, especially regarding the use of quilts as secret codes, does cast enough doubt on the methods of communication to warrant the use of the term *probably*.

Accordingly, teachers will want to emphasize the important distinction between the myth and the reality of the Underground Railroad with students. Encourage them to think about the letters they write to friends. How do they try to portray themselves, their achievements and/or shortcomings, to a close friend? What kinds of biases do they bring to their letter writing? Have they ever written a confidential letter or kept a diary in a secret code to prevent someone else from gaining sensitive knowledge? How will grandchildren or great-grandchildren interpret their writings years from now? These are the kinds of issues that will give students a better appreciation for the secrecy as well as questionable accuracy of documents regarding the Underground Railroad and why it is important to speculate about a letter writer's intention rather than to state it as fact.

Finally, this student's identification of the letter's importance—its revelation of "how the Underground Railroad operated between Wilmington, Delaware, where Garrett lived, and Philadelphia, where Still lived" and "that both of these men were good friends who put their lives at risk to help runaway slaves"—is precisely the kind of lesson students should learn from this exercise.

Another letter taken from Still's book, shown on the following page, offers a more cryptic description of the manner in which the Underground Railroad operated.[11]

Washington, D.C., June 22, 1854

MR. WILLIAM STILL: —Sir—I have just received a letter from my friend, William Wright, of York Sulphur Springs, Pa., in which he says, that by writing to you, I may get some information about the transportation of some property from this neighborhood to your city or vicinity.

A person who signs himself Wm. Penn, lately wrote to Mr. Wright, saying he would pay $300 to have this service performed. It is for the conveyance of only one small package; but it has been discovered since, that the removal cannot be so safely effected without taking two larger packages with it. I understand that the three are to be brought to this city and stored in safety, as soon as the forwarding merchant in Philadelphia shall say he is ready to send on. The storage, etc., here, will cost a trifle, but the $300 will be promptly paid for the whole service. I think Mr. Wright's daughter, Hannah, has also seen you. I am also known to Prof. C.D. Cleveland, of your city. If you answer this promptly, you will soon hear from Wm. Penn himself.

Very truly yours,
J. BIGELOW, ESQ.

STUDENT INTERPRETATION

This primary source is a letter written to William Still. While the letter appears to be about a package and merchants, these are probably metaphors for slaves, stations and conductors on the Underground Railroad. The author informs William Still that a man who writes under the name "William Penn" will pay $300 to have three slaves transported to safety, and also to seek his help.

The author signs as J. Bigelow, Esq. The "Esq." means "esquire" or "gentleman." Since lawyers use that title, Bigelow was probably a lawyer. He is against slavery, but does not write like a conductor. He is very formal in the letter where other letters from conductors to William Still call him "friend" and are more casual. Therefore, Bigelow is someone who doesn't regularly help runaways, but may be helping a friend who is an Underground Railroad agent. One key sentence is, "I am also known to Prof. C.D. Cleveland, of your city." If Bigelow knew Still, he would not have needed to identify himself in this way.

Bigelow writes from Washington D.C. where slavery was legal, even though it was close to free states. It was not a popular place to hide slaves, which also supports that this was not an ordinary case.

This document is important not only because it helps to give three people their freedom, but because it shows that even people who were not directly involved with the Underground Railroad were sympathetic to that cause.

This student does an impressive job of interpreting an extremely challenging letter. He identifies the use of commercial vocabulary as a metaphor for escaping slaves. Thus, he explains that the runaways are referred to as "packages" to be "conveyed" from Washington, D.C., to Philadelphia "as soon as the forwarding merchant," or stationmaster, "shall say he is ready to send [them] on." Just as important, the student correctly identifies the author of the letter, J. Bigelow, as a lawyer assisting a friend, William Wright, who was an agent. Such individuals were referred to on the Underground Railroad as a "friend of a friend." What tipped the student off was Bigelow's "formal" writing style, which is not like the "more casual" style of other conductors who refer to William Still as "friend." Additionally, the student points out that Bigelow feels it necessary to mention a mutual acquaintance, Prof. C. D. Cleveland, in order to gain Still's trust.

Those students who may find the concept of cryptic language difficult might be encouraged to write their own code letters, using a secretive vocabulary that they are more comfortable with. Ask them to provide a vocabulary key or definitions for the code words at the end of the letter. This method of learning by doing is often helpful for students who have difficulty with abstract thinking skills.

Although individuals like Bigelow were not active participants on the Underground Railroad, they were critical to the operation of the enterprise. They served as important liaisons, especially in cases where the local stationmasters or conductors were illiterate and could not communicate directly with Still. Sometimes they also provided the finances necessary for transportation to the North.[12] The student grasped this significant point in the final line of his essay, indicating that the letter "shows that even people who were not directly involved with the Underground Railroad were sympathetic to that cause."

The letter contains one other important reference to the operation of the Underground Railroad, though it eluded the student: runaway children rarely, if ever, escaped alone. Children, like single women, were almost always accompanied by one or more adult males.[13] Bigelow registers this point in his reference to "only one small package" whose "removal cannot be so safely effected without taking two larger packages with it."

Another way to teach students how to interpret primary source letters is to have them write their own. The following student was asked to read a series of four letters, including the two just discussed, and then write her own, requesting assistance in aiding a runaway slave in such a manner that someone intercepting it would not know what it was about. After reading the letters, the student made a list of all the code words contained in the letters. She identified the following code words: *trips of mercy to God's poor* (helping runaways escape to freedom in the North); *special agent* (God); *poor, worthless wretches* (slave catchers); *Moses* (Harriet Tubman); and *packages* (runaway slaves). Then she wrote the following letter:

Wilmington, 8th Mo. 2nd, 1860

Dear Friend, William Still,

On the 30th of 7th Month, I had a dream that Moses sent me five of God's poor. Moses told me that each of God's poor needs help in escaping to the Promised land. I said that I would help them. I will notify you on how my dream turns out.

Today, six packages arrived at my house. I told the delivery man that I will give the packages to a friend of mine in Kennett, Isaac Mendenhall. I also told him that I have a special agent helping me and that the packages will be delivered safely. The man asked that I tell him when the packages, especially the smallest one, are delivered to their new home. I told him I would.

Your dear friend,
Thomas

This student does several impressive things in her letter. First, she demonstrates her understanding of nineteenth-century Quaker etiquette by dating the letter "8th Mo. 2nd, 1860" and then identifying, in the letter, July 30 of that same year as "30th of 7th Month." She also addresses William Still as "Dear Friend," also a Quaker custom. Second, she demonstrates her understanding not only of code words but also of the religious nature of those words. Her use of "Moses" refers to Harriet Tubman, who was often called the Moses of her people because, like Moses of the Old Testament, who led the Jews out of bondage in Egypt, Tubman led black slaves out of bondage in the South.[14]

Similarly, the student uses "God's poor" to refer to runaways and "Promised land" as a reference to freedom in the North. While all Underground Railroad agents used the vocabulary of the railroad to disguise the true meaning of this illegal route to freedom, Quakers also used religious language, probably as a reminder that their involvement, though illegal according to civil law, was consistent with God's law. Finally, the student demonstrates her knowledge of the types of runaways who escaped on the Underground Railroad, noting that the "packages" to be delivered were not just adults, but children, a point she makes by referring to the "smallest" package and the concern she has that it is delivered safely to its "new home."

Summary

Regardless of the document, public declarations, diaries, newspaper advertisements, and letters are the stuff of history. Although they present a particular bias held at a particular period of time, documents also bring students face-to-face with the actual words and thoughts of the stationmasters, conductors, and, sometimes, former slaves who shaped the Underground Railroad. In the process, documents can help students understand the human element of history, personalizing it in a way that no textbook can. In Chapter 3, we will explore two other types of primary source documents: photographs and engravings.

Endnotes

1. John Hope Franklin, *The Emancipation Proclamation* (New York: Doubleday & Co., Inc., 1963); and David H. Donald, *Lincoln* (New York: Simon and Schuster, 1995).

2. John Hope Franklin and Loren Schweninger, *Runaway Slaves: Rebels on the Plantation* (New York: Oxford University Press, 1999), 213–14.

3. Ibid., 210–11.

4. Ibid., 210–13; and Billy G. Smith and Richard Wojtowicz, *Blacks Who Stole Themselves: Advertisements for Runaways in the* Pennsylvania Gazette, *1728–1790* (Philadelphia: University of Pennsylvania Press, 1989), 13.

5. Franklin and Schweninger, *Runaway Slaves*, 212.

6. Ibid., 214–15.

7. Howard Brinton, *Friends for 300 Years* (Wallingford, PA: Pendle Hill, 1976), pp. 134–38.

8. William Still, *The Underground Railroad* (1872) (Chicago: Johnson, 1970 reprint), xiii.

9. Benjamin Quarles, "Foreword," in William Still, *The Underground Railroad* (1872) (Chicago: Johnson, 1970 reprint), v.

10. Still, *Underground Railroad*, 554–55.

11. Ibid., 22–23.

12. James A. McGowan, *Station Master on the Underground Railroad: The Life and Letters of Thomas Garrett* (Moylan, PA: Whimsie, 1977), 5.

13. Franklin and Schweninger, *Runaway Slaves*, 63–66, 213.

14. See Sarah Bradford, *Harriet Tubman: The Moses of Her People* (1986) (Bedford, MA: Applewood, 1993 reprint), 3–4. Garrett had a special relationship with Harriet Tubman, whom he often referred to as Moses. She was probably the most frequent visitor to his station in Wilmington, Delaware, and he spoke highly of her in his letters to William Still. (See McGowan, *Station Master*, 89–90).

Chapter Three

Imagining the Railroad
Teaching with Photographs and Engravings

Photographs and engravings are among the most fascinating primary sources. Students, especially visual learners, can relate with the human element revealed by them. In addition, the stories revealed by photographs and engravings tend to stimulate a youngster's imagination, especially during the middle school years. Images of the past enable students to imagine people or conditions other than those that exist in contemporary society. Historical images of slavery and abolitionism encourage students to visualize those subjects and then move beyond the images by writing about them. The challenge for the teacher is to constantly ensure that the curriculum allows for students to think about the possible as well as the actual. But that can occur only if we understand the developmental characteristics of the middle schooler and how they apply to his or her imaginative behavior.[1]

First, preadolescents are readily engaged by stories that appeal to their emotions. Among the most fascinating archetype is the heroic journey, which can be fitted to many varied situations and events.[2] For example, we can tell the story of a daring escape or a courageous rescue to introduce the Underground Railroad to students not just as a historical event but as a powerfully plotted tale that embodies the actions of a heroine like Harriet Tubman. The story begins, however, with an image that will pique student curiosity.

Second, middle school students are also at a point in their development where there is growing ambivalence toward authority. On one hand, they seek to resist or challenge the adult world, and on the other, they are trying to find a place in it.[3] There are tensions and conflicts that arise as middle school students navigate this transition from reliance on the adult world to their own independence. Often the tensions can be seen in their idealism and easily stimulated sense of injustice, which leads to revolt. They tend to express ideals of how the world should work and often become disturbed by the injustice when it fails to meet those ideals. Middle school students also experiment with ideal roles for themselves as their imaginations allow them to think through all the possibilities. Sometimes those roles allow them to revolt against the prevailing conventions of the adult world.[4] The image of a runaway slave's scarred back, the result of a severe whipping, evokes that sense of injustice, just as a photograph of a defiant abolitionist jailed for his role in a daring escape in violation of the federal fugitive slave law might evoke feelings of justified revolt.

Finally, middle school students are willing to investigate the details of a topic when they are interested in it. They are becoming increasingly aware of the complexity of society, both of the past and of the present, and tend to pay careful attention to matters of detail.[5] This behavior can easily be made part of the student's imaginative engagement with the Underground Railroad through photographs and engravings, which require the skills of careful observation, discernment, and critical thinking.

These three behavioral patterns give middle school students a natural affinity for interpreting photographs and engravings associated with slavery, abolitionism, and the Underground Railroad.

The Significance of Photography in America

Photography was one of the most important inventions of the nineteenth century. For the first time it was possible to know the exact appearance of people, objects, and events that could not be viewed before. The first photograph appeared in 1839 and was called a *daguerreotype*, an image formed on a silver-coated copper plate. The daguerreotype appeared so lifelike that it was called a "mirror with a memory." Whereas the painter could romanticize a person's features, the daguerreotype told the truth—for better or worse. Nevertheless, daguerreotypes became so popular that it seemed everyone wanted to be immortalized.

By the 1850s, the development of the glass plate negative allowed for multiple copies of a photograph to be made. The daguerreotype became obsolete and a new form, the *carte de visite*, appeared. The Civil War generated an even greater demand for photographs, especially portraits of the common soldier. These images recorded for posterity a moment of great pride in the life of the subject.[6] Appearance, posture, and clothing are all significant elements in studying the subject of a historical photograph. Facial expression and the person's pose in relation to the camera lens, in particular, were important clues to the kind of impression a subject wanted to convey about his character. Smiling, for example, was not popular as it suggested frivolity or a lack of seriousness. Staring directly into the camera expressionless, on the other hand, suggested forthrightness and honesty. Gazing away from the lens suggested thoughtfulness in a man and modesty in a woman.

Just as pose and expression revealed a person's character, clothing often described her social status. Props were also used to convey a subject's wealth or accomplishments. Books, for example, indicated a good education or a scholarly bent. Additional rules applied for group portraits. The most important person dominated the photo by being placed at its focal point, with others surrounding that person a slight distance away as a sign of respect. The dominant person might also be seated while others stood. This is especially the case in family portraits, in which the male head of the house reminded the viewer of patriarchal authority. Gestures of affection were unusual because it was not acceptable to show such emotions in public.[7]

Photographs are among the most useful sources for studying history because they can re-create the atmosphere of a time period, indicate styles of clothing during a particular era, and reveal insight into an individual's personality. But to use photographs effectively as a research tool, a student must have some background knowledge of history to analyze them. The amount of evidence as well as the type of evidence that can be extracted from a photograph will depend on how much a student already knows about the topic. The more background knowledge a student has, the richer the photograph becomes as a source.

A Model for Analyzing Photographs

How do you read a photograph? Much like a book: from left to right, then from top to bottom. Break down the photo into smaller components (e.g., background, foreground, groups of objects or people) and examine each one carefully. Review the photograph several times, trying to identify something you might have missed each time. Ask yourself some general questions about the action(s), people, buildings, or event being portrayed. In order to think through these issues, I provide students with the following checklist for each photograph:

First reactions: Jot down whatever first impressions you get about the photograph itself and the persons or objects in the photo. Describe your feelings.

Detailed examination: List all the observable facts in the photo (i.e., people, objects, actions).

Facts known from other sources: Indicate here the actual place and date of the photograph if not on the photo itself, the names of the people portrayed, and so on.

Characteristic expression or special relationships of persons or objects in the photograph: Is the subject staring into the camera lens or away from it? Is there any noticeable expression? If so, how do you characterize it?

Describe the mood of the photograph: Formal, candid, happy, unhappy, indifferent. Explain your response.

Considered reactions: Jot down how you feel about the photograph now that you've studied it carefully and answered any questions you may have had.

Now let's look at an example. Figure 3–1 is an 1848 daguerreotype of the African American abolitionist Frederick Douglass. This is a rare daguerreotype because it is one of the very few images of Douglass as a young man. Over the last decade the image has captured the interest of Ken Burns and other producers of historical documentaries. Because of that interest, the image has appeared on several Public Broadcasting Station programs on the Civil War, the Mexican-American War, and, more recently, a series on Abraham Lincoln. The narrators of those documentaries point out that Douglass' distant gaze and formal attire as well as the careful grooming of his hair all indicate that the former slave was trying to convey the impression of a middle-class gentleman. His skin complexion, which is accentuated by the light source, makes him almost indistinguishable from a white man, reinforcing this impression. This kind of interpretation has led many viewers to speculate that Douglass was trying to disprove white notions about the intellectual inferiority of antebellum African Americans.

However, further investigation of the history behind the daguerreotype offers another explanation.

According to the provenance of this artifact, Douglass had the daguerreotype taken sometime around the year 1848 to give as a gift to Susan B. Anthony, a white Quaker reformer who championed abolitionism and women's rights. He had met Anthony in Rochester, New York, where her family lived. Douglass had settled in Rochester a year earlier to begin publishing an antislavery newspaper titled the *North Star*. The image was originally contained in a small leather case and framed by a brass mat and was intended to be held in the hand by its viewer. It is also an intimate likeness rather than an ennobling one, meant to be given to a close friend or loved one, not intended for public display.[8] Could it be that Douglass longed for intimacy with Susan B. Anthony? If so, Douglass' expression may be interpreted as one of sadness because the moral conventions of antebellum America restricted his choices, in this case, the choice to court and possibly marry a white woman. Or perhaps the daguerreotype is simply a powerful illustration of a close friendship that transcended the boundaries of race and gender, something that was extremely rare in antebellum society. Whatever the

Figure 3–1. *Frederick Douglass (ca. 1848). The purpose of this photograph of a young Frederick Douglass remains a mystery.*

case might have been, the Douglass daguerreotype demonstrates the necessity of acquiring some background knowledge before interpreting the subject's intended meaning.

Analyzing Antebellum Photographs

The model provided in the previous section was used by middle school students to interpret the next three photographs. Figure 3–2 is a well-known image of Harriet Tubman, the most famous conductor of the Underground Railroad. Born into slavery on a Maryland plantation in 1820, Tubman first attempted to escape at age seven, but was caught, severely beaten, and put to work as a field laborer. Some twenty years later, she succeeded in escaping to the North and began her involvement with the Underground Railroad. Between 1850 and 1860, she is said to have returned to the South on nineteen separate occasions to

Figure 3–2. *Harriet Tubman (ca. 1845). Tubman's middle-class appearance refutes the popular white notion of black inferiority.*

guide more than three hundred slaves, including her parents, to freedom. In the process, she earned for herself the name Moses of her people, after the Old Testament prophet who led the Jews out of bondage in Egypt.[9]

If they studied the topic in elementary school, most middle school students will have some knowledge of Tubman and the folklore associated with her. The following is a typical student interpretation of the photo.

STUDENT INTERPRETATION 1

First reactions: The photo looks like it was painted. The black woman in the photo seems formal.

Detailed examination: The woman is middle-aged, maybe about thirty or forty years old. She is wearing a long dress with a button-down shirt and a scarf around her neck. Her hair is braided. She is standing with her hands on the end of a sofa. There is a table behind her.

Facts known from other sources: I know that the woman is Harriet Tubman because I've seen this picture before.

Describe the mood of the photograph: The expression on the woman is very dull. There is no smile. It is a formal pose.

Considered reactions: Harriet Tubman looks like she is living a comfortable life as a free person in the North. She enjoys the same kind of clothing and lifestyle as any middle-class white person.

The student does a nice job of moving from concrete observations—pose, physical description of Tubman, and objects—to a more abstract hypothesis, specifically that "Harriet Tubman looks like she is living a comfortable life as a free person in the North" and that she "enjoys the same kind of clothing and lifestyle as any middle-class white person." He admits that he has "seen this picture before" and therefore knows that it is Tubman. Although these observations don't seem very insightful, they serve as a good entry point for a class discussion on why students would make the identification between freedom and a middle-class lifestyle in antebellum America. More motivated students might be asked to consider why nineteenth-century whites doubted the ability of former slaves to assimilate into mainstream society given Tubman's middle-class appearance in the photograph.

Another student used her initial interpretation of the photograph to write a creative story about Tubman:

STUDENT INTERPRETATION 2

Harriet Tubman was like Moses. In fact, many people called her that. Harriet Tubman deserved the name Moses, and the honor that it signified. Harriet was a slave for a good portion of her life. She was born a slave in Maryland around 1820. No one knows the exact date because slaves' birth dates were rarely recorded.

When Harriet was only six years old she was sent out to work because, to her owner, she was a problem child. Harriet, as a child, was often beaten for doing her chores incorrectly. One day Harriet ran away, to get away from the harsh treatment and life of a slave. She lived in a pigpen for a very short while, but then became so hungry that she had to return to her owner. Harriet was beaten very badly for daring to flee, but that didn't stop her good mood.

While she was a child, Harriet was a hard worker. As she became older, her sisters were sold away into the Deep South. One day, Harriet was hit in the head with a rock when she didn't stop a slave from running away. From that point on, Harriet often fell asleep while doing her tasks. In order to avoid being sold, Harriet made sure that she fell asleep every time a slave seeker came around since no one wanted a slave that fell asleep all the time.

Then Harriet decided to try to run away again. This time she was older, and alone. She took no one with her since she had tried to run away before with her brothers, and they all got captured. Harriet promised herself that she would return for her family, and she left. Harriet returned time and again to bring slaves out of the South into the free states.

This picture was taken right after Harriet helped her first fifty slaves escape. She had this picture taken to commemorate the day. She was a conductor on the Underground Railroad, and it shows in this picture. Harriet looks worn out and tired from all of her hard work. Harriet also looks kind of sad and very serious due to what a hard life she led while she was a slave. In this picture it shows that Harriet was slowly obtaining wealth, and that she was free.

"I am amazed and proud of myself that I was able to save so many slaves," Harriet thought as she stood there posing for the picture. "Now I have to save even more slaves. I want them to be able to live a good life like the one that I am living now, even if it does mean risking my life to save them. They don't deserve to be treated horribly because they are black, and I want to do even more to help stop it. I wish I could find my two sisters and save them since I helped the rest of my family escape, but I don't think that there is much hope in finding them since we are so far apart right now. All I know is that I am meant to help people get the freedom that they deserve, and I plan on doing that until the day I die."

After this picture was taken, Harriet decided that she had to keep trying to help slaves no matter what. She didn't care what it would take. With much courage, Harriet managed to help a total of 300 slaves escape to freedom in the North. This was an amazing accomplishment considering the number of people looking for her, and that a reward was being offered for her capture.

Although this student didn't cover all the issues requested in the photo assessment checklist, her analysis of the photograph was more creative than those of her classmates. Of special interest is her statement at the beginning of the essay that "Harriet Tubman deserved the name Moses, and the honor that it signified." The placement of this sentence at the beginning of the essay as well as the subsequent information the student offers to support it serves as a thesis for the piece and shows how easily a photo analysis can be adapted to a writing exercise. To be sure, the essay proceeds more like a chronological narrative of Tubman's life rather than the kind of thematically organized essay expected at the high school level. At the same time, however, the student does offer some good, keen insight that is reflective of a more advanced stage of writing. For example, she quickly clarifies her statement that Harriet was "born a slave in Maryland *around* 1820" with the claim that "no one knows the exact date because slaves' birth dates were rarely recorded." In so doing, she demonstrates the point that missing data is common when dealing with the history of slavery. Similarly, the student makes an important connection between Harriet's middle-class lifestyle, as shown by her dress and surrounding objects in the photograph, and freedom. After noting that Harriet was "slowly obtaining wealth, and that she was free," the student writes that Tubman was motivated to help slaves, in part, so that they could "live a good life like the one that [she was] living now." What's more, she uses the first-person style to convey the point, adding to reader interest as well as the persuasiveness of the insight.

At the same time, the student delivers some rather puzzling insights that reflect the candor and/or innocence of the middle school age. For example, her observation that Harriet "lived in a pigpen for a very short while" underscores the student's attempt to show the truly dismal living conditions of slaves, though few of us would use the term "pigpen" out of respect for the human beings who were subjected to those conditions. An example of the student's innocence is revealed by her insight that though "Harriet was beaten very badly for daring to flee," the beating still "didn't stop her good mood." At first glance, a teacher might interpret the observation as an insult, as if to say that Tubman didn't know any better. But when the remark is placed in the broader context of the essay, it becomes clear that Tubman's positive disposition was yet another form of rebellion. That is, she refused to allow the treatment of her master, no matter how abusive it might have been, to get the best of her. While these statements might be politically incorrect, they can be used by teachers as a valuable opportunity to discuss the importance of vocabulary, especially in regard to racially sensitive topics like slavery and the Underground Railroad.

Now let's take a look at a photograph that is more complicated to interpret. Figure 3–3 depicts the 1855 imprisonment of Passmore Williamson, a

Figure 3–3. *Passmore Williamson in Moyamensing Prison, Philadelphia (1855). Williamson's crossed arms and his direct stare into the camera suggest his personal defiance of the 1850 Fugitive Slave Law.*

white Quaker abolitionist who was arrested for helping three slaves escape from a ship in Philadelphia. Their owner demanded Williamson either return the slaves or compensate him for his loss. When he refused, Williamson was prosecuted and jailed at Philadelphia's Moyemensing Prison. As the case gained notoriety, Williamson was visited in his cell by several notable abolitionists, including Frederick Douglass and Harriet Tubman. One of those visitors was a daguerreotypist, who took the photo to publicize the unjust nature of Williamson's imprisonment. The student who wrote the following interpretation wasn't given any of this information before he completed his assessment of the photograph.

STUDENT INTERPRETATION

First reactions: The man in the photo seems to be using an intentional pose. It's hard to really tell where he is, whether it's a home or an office. There aren't enough details to really distinguish the location.

Detailed examination: The man is formally dressed with a bow tie. He has long side burns and he seems to be in his 40s. He is sitting with his hands across his body. He must be sitting on a chair, although you can't see it. The only object in the photo looks like a window with bars.

Facts known from other sources: None

Characteristic expression: The man in the photo doesn't seem to have any special relationship to the window and there are no other people in the photograph.

Describe the mood of the photograph: The man seems to be smiling and his body position, with his arms folded across his stomach seems to say that he's proud of himself. The mood of the photo is kind of gloomy and dark.

Considered reactions: I think the man might be a lawyer who is standing outside of a jail. What I thought was a window with bars might be the door to a jail cell. Maybe the lawyer has just put a criminal in jail and is proud of it.

As I mentioned before, this is an *extremely* difficult photograph for a middle school student to interpret. Most of the background setting has been cropped, making it difficult to see that the bars are indeed the door to a prison cell. The student's comment that "it's hard to really tell where [Williamson] is" because "there aren't enough details to really distinguish the location" is evidence of that fact. Instead, the daguerreotypist intended to focus the viewer's attention on Williamson and his defiant pose. The image was an important piece of propaganda designed to publicize the injustice of the Quaker abolitionist's imprisonment. Nevertheless, the student, upon further investigation of the photo, identifies Williamson's "intentional pose" with "his arms folded across his stomach" as an indication that he is "proud of himself." He also correctly identifies the "window with bars" as "the door to a jail cell," though he makes Williamson out to be a "lawyer who is standing outside" of that door, rather than a prisoner seated inside the cell.

What is important here is that the student has used his imagination as well as his deductive and/or inductive reasoning to create a hypothetical story. Once the interpretation was completed, the teacher gave the student the actual facts of Williamson's imprisonment to show just how close the student came to discerning those facts on his own.

One more photo analysis will show just how creative some students are as they contemplate these images, especially in the absence of any prior knowledge of the photograph. Figure 3–4 is a daguerreotype of Gordon, a runaway slave from Mississippi, who was photographed by a medical inspector when he joined the Union Army in 1863. Very little is known about Gordon, the medical inspector, or even the nature of the physical exam. But apparently, the inspector was shocked to discover the network of scars on the former slave's back, the result of several whippings he endured during his bondage. The following student essay is titled "A Picture Is Worth 1,000 Words."

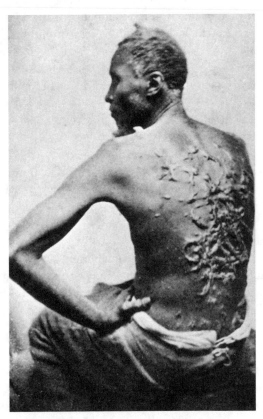

Figure 3–4. *Gordon, runaway slave (ca. 1863). The network of scars on Gordon's back reflects the brutal inhumanity of slavery.*

STUDENT INTERPRETATION

My picture is that of a 30 year-old man named Jim. Jim had two children, a girl Lynn, 5, and a boy, Sam, 12. He was married to a lady named Eliza. They luckily lived together, but sadly they lived together on a Louisiana plantation and worked as slaves.

Jim's owner was very cruel. A brutal beating follows everything done wrong, even if it's very minor. In fact on Jim's plantation a couple of people have died after a beating. Jim gets whipped a lot and wants it to stop. He dreams of living freely with his family in Canada.

Before this picture was taken, Jim made a very hard decision. He decided to run away, leaving his family behind. He left them behind because the last time he tried to run away with them, they were caught and beaten badly, 500 lashes! He left at night, running as fast as he could. He finally got to the Ohio River, where he met a man named Sean. Sean offered to take Jim to the other side and freedom. He finally arrived at Levi Coffin's house in Cincinnati. Levi was a conductor on the Underground Railroad. He asked Jim if he could take a picture of his back, which showed all the scars from the whippings he suffered. Jim agreed.

As Jim sat there, he couldn't help ponder what would happen to him next:

"I wonder if this picture will get back to my owner, and if it does, will he look for me?

Will he use the picture to ask people if they've seen me?

Will I ever see my family again?

I wonder how they are, especially Sam. He had a horrid cough before I left. Oh and my poor Eliza, she's probably getting horrible beatings! Without me there to give her some of my cotton, she doesn't pick near enough to please the master. And my baby girl, Lynn, I wonder if she's learned anything new since I left. Oh how I long to see them!

I hope I make it to Canada.

After the picture was taken, Levi directed Jim to a nearby station. Before he left, Jim asked Levi to try and save his family and help them to Canada. Jim traveled north to Canada where he finally go a job and a home. After five years, his dream finally came true. He was now reunited with his family and living as a free man.

While the essay does not develop the few facts we know about Gordon, it does reflect the great imagination of the middle schooler who wrote it and demonstrates the experience of a runaway by giving him a personal identity. This fictional approach is one way to appeal to those students who have a personal strength in storytelling. Teachers should encourage creativity and flexibility in writing, as long as students are made to understand that history itself must be based on documentary evidence or proven fact. If not, the treatment is *historical fiction*, that is, a story that is broadly based on historical events but cannot be substantiated, point-for-point, with documentary evidence.

Having said that, I was especially impressed by this student's emphasis on the importance of family. As we've seen from the historiography, one of the major reasons a slave ran away was to prevent the separation of family or to be reunited with family. While Jim's situation does not fit either scenario, he is clearly devoted to his wife and his children as evidenced by the fact that during his first escape "he tried to run away with them" and "they were caught and beaten badly." But throughout the story, we read of Jim's concern for his wife and children, and before he takes leave of Levi Coffin, he even requests that the Quaker conductor "try and save his family and help them to Canada." Though we don't know how the family gets there, the student gives us the happy ending we hope for, namely that Jim made it to Canada and, five years later, "was . . . reunited with his family and living as a free man."

A Model for Analyzing Engravings

Engravings are more conducive to storytelling than photographs because the scenes they depict are more fluent than static. There is usually more than one subject and they are often interacting with each other. While teachers may want to use engravings as a method of encouraging their students to use their imaginations in a story-writing exercise, I prefer using engravings to spur critical thinking skills. I want the student to assume the role of a detective and examine carefully—and thoughtfully—the scene that is depicted, the interactions of the subjects, and any clues she may find to help her to establish the real story behind the scene. Therefore, I begin the exercise by having students complete the following questions as they examine the engraving and *before* I read them the narrative account of what actually took place:

1. *Who is shown in the engraving* (e.g., men, women, children)? List the people you see.
2. *What is the setting of the scene* (e.g., inside/outside, city/country)? How can you tell?
3. *What event or activity is taking place?* What are the people in the scene doing?
4. *Are there any tools, equipment, or other objects in the scene?* List the items you see. How are these items being used?
5. *What point or statement is the engraver (artist) trying to make?*

Only after students record their observations for these five questions will I read the actual account of the scene that is depicted. Then I ask students to record their *thoughtful reflections.*

Analyzing Engravings of the Underground Railroad

Figure 3–5 is a good example of an engraving that can elicit thoughtful student responses and valuable class discussions.

Here is the narrative account that I read to students after they record their initial observations of the engraving:

> As the clerk of the Pennsylvania Anti-Slavery Society's General Vigilance Committee, William Still had grown accustomed to surprises. Not only did the young free black abolitionist coordinate the Eastern Line of the Underground Railroad by finding shelter as well as an escape route to the North for fugitive slaves, but he recorded their stories of inhumane treatment by brutal owners, painful separations from family, and a passionate desire for freedom. Few of the stories, however, were as remarkable as the one that was about to unfold on a crisp autumn morning in 1848.

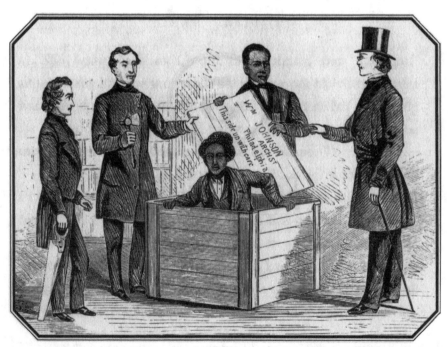

Figure 3–5. *Resurrection of Henry Box Brown. Engraving by T. Ellwood Zell (ca. 1870).*

Shortly after opening the doors of his office at 31 North Fifth Street in Philadelphia, Still was greeted by a fellow abolitionist and coworker, J. Miller McKim. McKim was standing beside a wooden packing crate that had been recently freighted from Richmond, Virginia. Although the crate was addressed to the Arch Street residence of William Johnson, McKim intercepted the box at the Philadelphia train station. Bound with five hickory hoops, the crate was two feet eight inches deep, two feet wide, and three feet long. On the lid were the words "This side up with care."

Still summoned two other abolitionists, Professor C. D. Cleveland and Lewis Thompson, and the four men pushed the crate inside the office. Then Still shuttered the windows and locked the door, while the others gathered around the wooden crate. Finally, McKim gently rapped on the lid of the box, inquiring, "All right in there?"

An answer came from within: "All right, sir!" Cleveland, with axe in hand, and Thompson, with a saw, cut the hickory hoops. Still lifted the lid, and out stepped Henry Brown, a runaway slave who, with the aid of a Richmond shoemaker, had had himself nailed inside the box and freighted to Philadelphia. All he had in his possession were a few biscuits, some water, and a small metal pick to poke air holes in the side of the box. After the grueling twenty-six-hour trip, some of which was spent upside down in the crate, Brown emerged with only a headache and was passed safely on to Boston.

News of the remarkable escape caused a sensation in the abolitionist newspapers, giving other slaves the same idea. Unfortunately for many of these would-be runaways, their crates became coffins as they died en route to the North.[10]

After reading the account, teachers may want to stimulate student thinking by asking the following questions: (1) Why was the crate sent to William Johnson? (2) How was Henry Brown able to survive a twenty-six-hour journey? and (3) What does this story and engraving tell you about the institution of slavery? These questions will not only serve to encourage students' thoughtful reflections of the engraving, but also form the basis of a class discussion after they have completed those reflections.

Here is how one student responded to the engraving. He wrote his thoughtful reflections after hearing the narrative account about the image.

STUDENT INTERPRETATION

1. *Who is shown in the engraving? List the people you see.* I see 3 white men along with two black men, one of whom is in a box.

2. *What is the setting of the scene? How can you tell?* This engraving is inside because you can see the floor boards and wall.

3. *What event or activity is taking place? What are the people in the scene doing?* These men have just opened the box, freeing the black man inside it. I can tell this because I see the axe and saw used to open the box.

4. *Are there any tools, equipment, or other objects in the scene? List the items you see. How are these items being used?* The men are standing around the box while the black man inside it looks as if he is ready to get out.

5. *What point or statement is the engraver (artist) trying to make?* The artist is trying to make the point that people will do anything to get free from slavery.

6. *Record your thoughtful reflections after the teacher has read you the actual account of what happened:* William Still is the black man holding the lid of the box. Henry Brown is the escaped slave inside of it. He was able to survive a 26 hour trip with only a few biscuits, some water and a small metal pick to poke air holes in the box. The other men are J. Miller McKim, a professor and Lewis Thompson, though I don't know which is which. The scene takes place in the fall of 1848. The box was sent to William Johnson as a decoy. This was probably to protect William Still. I think the artist is trying to tell us that slavery is horrible if slaves like Brown are willing to risk their lives and pack themselves in a box in order to get free.

The *Resurrection of Henry Box Brown* is a fine depiction of a runaway's desperation to escape. The student acknowledges this point in his statement that some "people will do anything to get free from slavery," and later, after hearing the narrative, he reinforces it with the observation "that slavery is horrible if slaves like Brown are willing to risk their lives and pack themselves in a box in order to get free." Teachers should tell students that the abolitionist press publicized the escape throughout the country with the result that many other slaves tried the same tactic. Unfortunately, many of the attempts resulted in death due to suffocation and exhaustion. Frederick Douglass, the free black abolitionist orator, became infuriated with the press for unnecessarily endangering the lives of fugitives for little more than bragging rights. He recognized that white abolitionists viewed the quest for freedom as a constitutional or abstract issue, whereas the black person saw it in much more personal terms. If white abolitionists could not understand the desperation Henry Brown felt when he risked his own life by having himself sealed in a wooden crate and freighted to freedom, then "it [was] time for those [slaves and former slaves] who suffered the wrong to lead the way [as abolitionists] in advocating liberty."[11]

The issue of the mailing address is also an interesting one. Notice that the student speculates that Brown's crate was sent to William Johnson "as a decoy" in order "to protect William Still" from being arrested for harboring a fugitive. It's a good insight, considering that no one knows for certain what the relationship was between Still and Johnson. All that is known is that the crate was intercepted by the Philadelphia Vigilance Committee at the city's train depot. This comment also shows that the student paid careful attention to a detail that might easily elude others.

Let's take a look at another engraving. Figure 3–6 is titled *The Christiana Tragedy* and is based on the following narrative:

> On the morning of September 11, 1851, Edward Gorsuch, a Baltimore slave owner, and a small party, including his son and a deputy U.S. marshal, laid in ambush at the home of William Parker in Christiana, Lancaster County, Pennsylvania. Like many of his neighbors, Parker was an active agent on the Underground Railroad and one who Gorsuch suspected of harboring three of his escaped slaves.
>
> According to the Fugitive Slave Law passed by Congress in 1850, Gorsuch was within his rights to recapture his escaped slaves with the assistance of a federal marshal. The law also levied fines and prison sentences

Figure 3–6. *The Christiana Tragedy. Engraving by T. Ellwood Zell (ca. 1870).*

on individuals like Parker who helped runaways and those who failed to assist in their capture. But when Gorsuch tried to gain entry to the house, Parker's wife sounded a horn to summon help. A band of neighbors responded to the call. They had grown accustomed to unscrupulous slave catchers intent on kidnapping the free black residents of Christiana and came armed and ready for a bloody confrontation.

Threats were exchanged. Castner Hanway, a Quaker miller, arrived on the scene to request the peaceful departure of the slave hunters. When the U.S. marshal tried to deputize the Quaker sympathizer, he refused, in violation of the Fugitive Slave Law. Instead, Hanway again pleaded with the slave hunters to leave. When it was clear that the blacks would not yield to their demands, Gorsuch's party began their attack. The blacks stood their ground, defending themselves with whatever weapons they could muster.

When the smoke cleared, the fugitives had escaped, Gorsuch was dead, his son was gravely injured, and the others had run off in fear. Parker, charged with treason, escaped to Canada on the Underground Railroad, insisting that Africans in the United States actually had "no country" because they enjoyed no protection under the law.[12]

STUDENT INTERPRETATION

1. *Who is shown in the engraving? List the people you see.* There is a small group of white men being chased by a larger group of black men.

2. *What is the setting of the scene? How can you tell?* The scene takes place outside in the country. I came to this conclusion because of the horse, the trees and what appears to be a field behind a fence. I also think that a big pile of hay can be seen in the background.

3. *What event or activity is taking place? What are the people in the scene doing?* It looks as if a small battle is occurring. Slaves are using farming tools as weapons to kill their white owners.

4. *Are there any tools, equipment, or other objects in the scene? List the items you see. How are these items being used?* Farming tools, like rakes and hoes are being used by the slaves. One of the slaves is firing a pistol.

5. *What point or statement is the engraver (artist) trying to make?* The artist is trying to make the point that just because you are treated unfairly by people and that those people may never be punished by society, doesn't mean that you deserve revenge.

This student does a nice job of inductive reasoning, as evidenced by her observation of the "country" setting and the "small battle" between "slaves" and their "white owners." Although most of the black subjects are, in fact,

free men, there were both former slaves and fugitives among them. It is difficult to determine exactly who all the figures are, but a few can be identified:
the dead body in the foreground is that of Edward Gorsuch, the Baltimore
slaveholder who came to capture his slaves; his son, Dixon, stands above
him, hand to forehead, having just been shot; and William Parker is at the
extreme left, holding the pistol. Taken as a whole, the student's assumption is
fairly accurate.

What is most interesting about this assessment, though, is her interpretation of the significance: "just because you are treated unfairly by people
and that those people may never be punished by society, doesn't mean that
you deserve revenge." The student changed her mind about this "turn the
other cheek" perspective after she read the narrative and considered the following questions: (1) Why did Parker and his neighbors resort to violence
when they knew they were breaking the law? (2) Why did Castner Hanway
refuse to be deputized when he knew he was breaking the law? and (3) What
do the story and the engraving tell you about the beliefs and methods of the
abolitionists? In her thoughtful reflections, the student wrote: "After hearing the story of Christiana, I think the reason it was a tragedy was because
even after they escaped to the North Parker and the other fugitives were not
really free and had to defend themselves from being captured and taken back
to slavery." The exercise of having to reconsider her views after reading the
actual account of Christiana was an important lesson in empathy building
for this middle schooler. Although I do not know if this particular student
was African American or white, I do think that students of both races can
become sensitized to their own biases as well as the different perspectives of
others by completing such an interpretive lesson.

In addition, the Christiana event teaches students about some of the
popular misconceptions about the time period. Contrary to popular belief,
nineteenth-century African Americans were not passive observers or recipients of white abolitionist efforts to achieve emancipation. Black resistance
took many forms, including armed resistance. Christiana ranks with the Nat
Turner slave rebellion of 1831 as one of the major revolts in African American history and, along with John Brown's 1859 raid at Harper's Ferry, served
as a harbinger of the Civil War.[13] The Christiana resistance emboldened such
black abolitionists as Robert Purvis and Frederick Douglass to issue pro-
nouncements of redemptive violence.

"Should any wretch enter my dwelling to execute this fugitive slave law
on me or mine," declared Robert Purvis at the Pennsylvania Antislavery Society's annual meeting held at West Chester on October 17, 1851, "I'll seek the
life of that pale-faced spectre, I'll shed his blood!"[14] Similarly, Frederick Douglass went so far as to argue the "rightfulness of forcible resistance." Urging

free blacks to arm themselves in an 1853 address, the famous black orator insisted that "the only way to make the Fugitive Slave Law a dead letter [was] to make a half dozen or more dead kidnappers."[15]

Both Purvis and Douglass were expressing the willingness of African Americans to resort to force in order to gain the fundamental rights of citizenship. Their common frustration as well as the bloody resistance at Christiana reflected the alienation blacks felt in a nation that was unwilling to ensure their rights as human beings. This is an important lesson for students, both black and white, to learn if they are to become informed citizens in a multicultural society that seeks to redress social injustice when it arises.

The final engraving is titled *Rescue of Jane Johnson and Her Children* (Figure 3–7). Jane Johnson was the house servant of Colonel John H. Wheeler, a Southern slaveholder and recently named ambassador to Nicaragua. En route to his diplomatic appointment in July 1855, Wheeler, traveling to New York to board a passenger ship, passed through Philadelphia with Johnson and her two young sons.

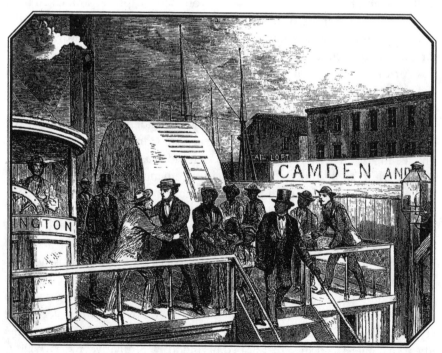

Figure 3–7. *Rescue of Jane Johnson and her children. Engraving by T. Ellwood Zell (ca. 1870).*

William Still learned of their arrival and of Johnson's desire for freedom. Still, along with Passmore Williamson, a white Quaker abolitionist, and a party of free black members of the Philadelphia Vigilance Committee, met them at the city's docks.

Still approached Johnson and said: "If you prefer freedom to slavery, as we suppose everybody does, you have the chance to accept it now. Act calmly—don't be frightened by your master—you are as much entitled to your freedom as we are, or as he is."

When the infuriated Wheeler tried to stop Johnson, the group of free black agents quickly gathered around him. Williamson placed his hands on the colonel to prevent him from seizing Johnson. A scuffle ensued as Still escorted Johnson and her sons to a waiting coach and transported them to his home.

For their actions in this daring rescue, Still and the others were charged with riot, forcible abduction, and assault. Wheeler also filed a civil suit, contending that the abolitionists violated the 1850 Fugitive Slave Law by "stealing" Johnson, his "property." He demanded that she be returned to him in accordance with the state law of Virginia.[16]

STUDENT INTERPRETATION

1. *Who is shown in the engraving? List the people you see.* There are men, a woman, and children. There are 12 men—8 are black and 4 are white.

2. *What is the setting of the scene? How can you tell?* The setting of the scene is a dock in Camden, New Jersey. You can tell by the sign that reads "Camden" in the background. Also, the people are on a steam boat. You can see the big wheel of the boat in the background and the steam coming out of the smoke stack.

3. *What event or activity is taking place? What are the people in the scene doing?* It looks like the woman and her children are leaving the boat with a black man. A white man with a beard is holding back another white man. They look like they're about to fight.

4. *Are there any tools, equipment, or other objects in the scene? List the items you see. How are these items being used?* The main object in this scene is the big steamboat, which people are trying to leave on. There is also a street lamp that is on, so it might be night time.

5. *What point or statement is the engraver (artist) trying to make?* The point the artist is trying to make is that the woman is trying to escape by boat and it is creating a conflict.

The student who wrote this analysis is very perceptive. She correctly notes that the scene is taking place in the area of Camden, New Jersey, which is located across the Delaware River from William Still's station at Philadelphia. She also gives us the details of the steamship, with its "big wheel" and "steam coming out of the smoke stack." Although she speculates incorrectly that Jane Johnson is "trying to escape by boat," she does note that the escape is "creating a conflict," as evidenced by the "white man with a beard [who] is holding back another white man" as if "they're about to fight."

Afterward, the student was asked to consider the following questions while reading the actual account: (1) Why did Johnson choose to escape in Philadelphia, instead of waiting to arrive in Nicaragua, where the government had abolished slavery by 1850? (2) Why did Wheeler file a criminal suit and a civil suit? and (3) What do the engraving and the story tell you about the legal status of a slave? After some thoughtful reflection, she wrote: "Jane Johnson showed a lot of courage and common sense. She knew that she had a better chance at getting freedom in Philadelphia than if she went to Nicaragua. But her escape caused a lot of legal problems. She was considered as a piece of property under the law. Her owner Colonel Wheeler had a right to sue William Still and the others for stealing his property. But Philadelphia was also in a free state. So Jane was also considered free. This story shows that the legal status of a slave at that time was very confusing."

Again, we can see how the narrative allows the student to move from the more concrete, factual description of the scene to a more abstract plane of thought. This interpretation reflects the kind of critical thinking done by some of the more insightful students. But any middle schooler should be able to glean one or two of these same points after reading the actual account of the Johnson rescue. Interestingly, none of the student writing samples mentioned the interracial nature of the rescue. I was hoping to read something about cooperation between white and black abolitionists because that interracial dimension is so critical to understanding the current fascination with the Underground Railroad. In the absence of such an important point, teachers should bring that observation to the attention of their students.

Incidentally, the Jane Johnson story has gained renewed interest because of the recent discovery of an unpublished original manuscript titled "The Bondswoman's Narrative, by Hannah Crafts, a Fugitive Slave." There are those scholars who believe that Jane Johnson herself penned the manuscript, using Hannah Crafts as a pseudonym.[17]

Summary

Photographs and engravings are among the most useful sources for studying antebellum history for middle school students. Not only do they re-create the atmosphere of the time period, but they also spark the imagination and pique the curiosity of the student and encourage further investigation. Teachers can enhance student interest by providing the necessary background information to help students draw insightful conclusions about the lifestyles, actions, and behaviors of those who participated on the Underground Railroad. Together, students and teachers can use photographs and engravings to become actively engaged in the process of *doing* historical research, rather than be passive observers.

Endnotes

1. See Kieran Egan, *Imagination in Teaching and Learning: The Middle School Years* (Chicago: University of Chicago Press, 1992). Egan argues that the period between the ages of eight and fifteen is an especially fertile age when teachers can appeal to the student's imaginative life to structure curriculum and pedagogy. He focuses on the characteristics of the typical middle schooler's imaginative life and how it can be engaged in the learning process in science, social studies, language arts, and mathematics.

2. Ibid., 75–82; and Kieran Egan, *Romantic Understanding: The Development of Rationality and Imagination, Ages 8–15* (New York: Routledge, 1990).

3. Patricia M. Spacks, *The Adolescent Idea: Myths of Youth and the Adult Imagination* (New York: Basic, 1981), 15.

4. Egan, *Imaginaton in Teaching and Learning*, 82–84.

5. Ibid., 84–86.

6. See Floyd Rinhart and Marion Rinhart, *The American Daguerreotype* (Athens: University of Georgia, 1981); William Welling, *Photography in America: The Formative Years, 1839–1900* (Albuquerque: University of New Mexico, 1978); and Beaumont Newhall, *The Daguerreotype in America* (New York: Dover, 1976).

7. Rinhart, *The American Daguerreotype.*, 28; and James G. Barber, "Who's Who?" *American Heritage* (July/August 1995): 76–86.

8. Pam Powell, "The Daguerreotype: Portraiture at the Dawn of Photography," in *The Daguerreian Annual,* ed. Mark S. Johnson (Pittsburgh, PA: Daguerreian Society, 2000).

9. See Sarah Bradford, *Harriet Tubman: The Moses of Her People* (1886) (Bedford, MA: Applewood, 1993 reprint).

10. See William Still, *The Underground Railroad* (1872) (Chicago: Johnson, 1970 reprint), 67–71; and Henry Brown, *Narrative of Henry Box Brown by Himself,* ed. George Stearns (Boston, 1849).

11. Frederick Douglass, *My Bondage and My Freedom* (1855) (New York: Dover, 1969 reprint), 404–6.

12. See Still, *Underground Railroad,* 360–71; and William Parker, "The Freedman's Story," *Atlantic Monthly* (February 1866): 154–66, and (March 1866): 281–87.

13. See Thomas Slaughter, *Bloody Dawn: The Christiana Riot and Racial Violence in the Antebellum North* (New York: Oxford University Press, 1991). For a more Afrocentric treatment, see Ella Forbes, *But We Have No Country: The 1851 Christiana Resistance* (Cherry Hill, NJ: Africana Homestead Legacy, 1998).

14. Robert Purvis quoted in *Pennsylvania Anti-Slavery Society Minutes:* October 17, 1851.

15. Douglass, *My Bondage and My Freedom,* 454–56.

16. See Still, *Underground Railroad,* 73–84. When Williamson refused to produce Johnson in court, a federal judge jailed him for contempt. At the trial of Still and five other blacks, Jane Johnson herself appeared and testified that she was not "kidnapped" but rather "went away at her own free will" and that she would "rather die than go back" to Wheeler. Still was acquitted, though two of the black men who assisted him served a week in jail for assault. Williamson, charged with "abducting slaves," was freed after three months in Philadelphia's Moyemensing Prison, where he became a *cause célèbre* for the abolitionist movement.

17. See Henry Louis Gates Jr., "The Fugitive," *The New Yorker Magazine* (February 18 and 25, 2002): 104–9, 111–16. In February 2001, Harvard scholar Henry Louis Gates, perusing the assorted lots of a New York City auction, discovered a historical gold mine—an unpublished original manuscript titled "The Bondswoman's Narrative by Hannah Crafts, a Fugitive Slave, recently Escaped from North Carolina." The 301-page manuscript, handwritten and clothbound, is a fictionalized biography in the genre of a slave narrative written during the 1850s. If, in fact, the account is based on the actual experience of a runaway slave, Gates had found the "first pristine encounter with the unadulterated voice of a fugitive, exactly as she wrote and edited it." Following his instincts, the Harvard professor purchased the manuscript and spent the next year authenticating its authorship. He now believes not only that the narrative was written by a fugitive slave, but that the author, Hannah Crafts, was in fact Jane Johnson, a house servant and participant in one of the most daring escapes on the Underground Railroad. "The Bondswoman's Narrative" is a compelling piece of history if it was written by a runaway slave at a time when literacy was considered the surest pathway from slavery to freedom. As such, it was illegal to educate blacks in the antebellum South. If Hannah Crafts is, as Henry Louis Gates believes, the real Jane Johnson, the manuscript offers historians some unique insight into the peculiar institution of slavery as well as into the history and operation of the Underground Railroad itself.

Chapter Four

Writing the Railroad
Local History Research Papers

Analyzing documents, photographs, and engravings and mastering factual content are critical to middle school students' understanding of the Underground Railroad. But those skills do not always allow them to see the broader context of the subject: the cause-and-effect relationship between the secret route to freedom and the larger abolitionist movement; the legal implications of the movement and how they influenced changes in both state and federal constitutions; and the cooperation that existed between black and white agents on a regional and sometimes national level. The most effective vehicle to build contextual understanding is a local history research paper.

Local history provides a wonderful avenue into the lives of ordinary people and the places where they lived, worked, and worshipped. It also excites middle school students. Because the local community is much like the family, it is less remote from the student's own interests and concerns; it is more concrete and easier to grasp. Students have a natural, vested interest in both the family and the local community, because they live within them. The events, behaviors, and rules in both institutions shape the middle school student's outlook, whether consciously or not. They also help define the way students look at the larger world and, in many ways, themselves. For these reasons, local history has great potential to demonstrate to students that the study of the past can be vitally and intrinsically exciting as well as relevant to their own lives. Because the Underground Railroad was a grassroots movement that was largely coordinated at the local level by abolitionist families, both black and white, the topic lends itself most readily to this kind of research paper.

Finally, local history provides middle school students with a firsthand experience of the past. In most schools the research paper, or term paper, is merely a review of the already existing scholarly interpretations of a particular subject of national significance. But at the higher levels of education, the purpose of doing a research paper is to advance new evidence or a new interpretation of a significant topic, which is often local in nature. The research, interpretation, and writing of the paper is, in a very real sense, "doing history." Middle schoolers are naturally attracted to learning by doing. In the process, many discover for the very first time the significance of the history that occurred in their own neighborhoods. They come to understand that historical research involves more than a visit to the public or school library; it also involves visiting special collections, museums, historical societies, and, in some cases, the historical site itself.

The Underground Railroad offers fertile ground for much research since it is a relatively new field of scholarship. Considering the voluminous literature in other fields of U.S. history, not much is known about the history, operation, and folklore of the secret route to freedom. Just think how exciting it would be for a middle school student to uncover some wholly new information that might contribute to this newly emerging scholarly field!

In Chapter 4, we will explore the guidelines and process of writing a local history research paper on the Underground Railroad and then analyze two examples of the kinds of papers that have been completed by middle school students.

As mentioned earlier, students residing in geographic areas that were not part of the Underground Railroad's history can still have a rewarding experience doing local history research on the topic. The websites provided in the bibliography can link a student to Underground Railroad station sites anywhere in the United States. Because of this technology, students in a location like Alaska can do research on the station of Levi Coffin, the so-called president of the Underground Railroad, who lived in Fountain City, Indiana. Some websites even have a virtual tour of the station site, which is almost as good as visiting the site in person.

Guidelines for the Research Paper

During the 2000–2001 school year, Chester County Historical Society partnered with a dozen schools to complete research on documented Underground Railroad sites in their school district. The sites were identified by Charles Blockson, a noted chronicler of the Underground Railroad, in his *Hippocrene Guide to the Underground Railroad*. Students were given the following guidelines:

1. Research papers must address either a documented Underground Railroad station or an underground railroad agent.
2. Papers must describe the importance of the person or the site to the Underground Railroad and explain how it relates to important events that took place during the time period 1800 to 1865.

3. Papers must explain what students have learned about race relations from their research and how we can apply that knowledge to race relations in our country today.

4. Papers must contain at least four bibliographic sources, two of which must be primary sources, and contain at least one photograph of the Underground Railroad site and/or the agent associated with it.

5. Students will observe the following process in the research and writing of the paper:
   - Identify site location and, if still standing, visit the site.
   - Identify libraries, special collections, and/or historical societies for information and visit them.
   - Find primary source documents relating to the site and/or agent and complete a Document Analysis Worksheet. (See Appendix A.)
   - Find a photograph relating to the site and/or agent and complete a Photo Analysis Worksheet. (See Appendix B.)
   - Collect three-by-five-inch note cards containing information on the site and/or agent.
   - Organize note cards into an outline.
   - Write a first draft based on the outline.
   - After reviewing teacher comments, complete the final draft.

   Each step of the process must be approved before students may go on to the next.

6. Papers must be typed, double-spaced, and a minimum of six pages, or about fifteen hundred words in length, not including endnotes, photographs, bibliography, or any appendices.

These guidelines integrate the interpretive skills introduced earlier in the book regarding documents and photographs and are designed to teach students accountability and to give them an understanding that good writing is a process that takes place over a period of weeks, months, or, often, many years' time; they are not designed to stifle creativity or put restraints on students' exploration of the topic.

This process took place over the course of a semester. Most teachers encouraged students to work in groups of three to four. Some of those groups were responsible for research, others for interpretation, and still others for the writing of the paper, though a certain degree of carryover was necessary. I find group projects to be best at the middle school level, especially when students have no previous experience with making note cards, drafting a bibliography, or writing a lengthy paper. There is much to be said about cooperative learning at this developmental level because it limits individual insecurity over the quality of work, creates a natural forum for the discussion of ideas within the group, and nurtures a sense of accountability to one's peers.

Where to Do Research

If students are to have a constructive experience with the research paper, teachers will have to provide them with the resources to ensure success. This can be done by directing students to the most helpful resources to begin their research and then identifying and contacting libraries, historical societies, and special collections in and near the school district. Geographic areas such as southeastern Pennsylvania, upstate New York, southwestern Ohio, Maryland, and Delaware enjoy a special history of Underground Railroad involvement and students who live in these areas will probably not have much difficulty finding material. But teachers in other parts of the country, where the Underground Railroad has not been clearly documented, will have to do more preparation.

Regardless of the geographic location, a good place for both students and teachers to begin their research is on the Web. Over the last few years, several websites dedicated to the Underground Railroad have been established. Among the very best is the National Park Service's "National Underground Railroad Network to Freedom" at *www.cr.nps.gov/ugrr*. This site offers valuable tips on how to research the Underground Railroad as well as contact information for Underground Railroad sites across the nation that have joined the Network to Freedom. Another valuable website was created by the National Underground Railroad Freedom Center in Cincinnati, Ohio. Located at *www.undergroundrailroad.com*, the Freedom Center's website offers a virtual tour of the Cincinnati-based museum, simulation exercises and curriculum for educators, tips on how to research an Underground Railroad site, and lists of all documented agents by county and state. Information about these and other websites can be found in the annotated bibliography at the end of this book.

Charles L. Blockson's *Hippocrene Guide to the Underground Railroad* (New York: Hippocrene, 1994) is a quick and easy reference to more than two hundred documented Underground Railroad sites across the country and can be found in most university libraries.

After exploring these more general sources, teachers will have to locate research institutions in their area. The middle school students whose work appears in this book completed their research at a variety of institutions ranging from large ones like the Philadelphia Free Library and the Historical Society of Delaware, to smaller regional organizations such as the Germantown Historical Society and the Underground Railroad sites themselves. Some of the more serious-minded students also visited special collections, such as the Quaker Collection of Haverford College Library and the Charles L. Blockson African American Collection at Temple University.

While special collections usually restrict admission to scholars and graduate and undergraduate students, middle school students may gain admission if they are accompanied by an adult and they phone ahead to schedule a time for their visit as well as inform the staff of their topic. If the permission is granted, students should plan to spend at least ninety minutes there taking notes. Most special collections also charge a fee since they are nonprofit organizations and the fees allow them to remain open.

Teachers would do well to emphasize these points with students before such a visit as they serve to limit student misunderstanding as well as teach young people the importance of stewardship of our cultural resources. Students also come to appreciate the fact that they are doing the work of a professional historian and on a topic that may very well have never before been explored!

Note Taking

Research usually begins with a supply of three-by-five-inch note cards that are used to take down information about the site or the agent, from both primary and secondary sources. One of the first obstacles a middle school student faces is how to determine what kind of information is important. At the outset, students should be encouraged to learn as much as possible about the topic by considering the following questions:

1. What is the time period of the subject?
2. What great events were happening in American history at the time?
3. What are the major highlights or events that took place at the site or in the life of the agent?
4. What is the importance of the site or the agent to the local community, state and/or nation?

These questions give students a framework in which they can gather information and, later, organize that information into an outline. At that point, teachers can offer constructive feedback, suggesting what areas need more research.

Another common frustration for students is deciding what information should be quoted and what should be paraphrased. Although it's impossible to give specific directions for making that decision, students should consider the following points. First, is the author's wording especially effective? If so, use it. For example, President Abraham Lincoln's Gettysburg Address begins: "Four score and seven years ago, our fathers brought forth upon the face of this continent, a new nation conceived in liberty, and dedicated to the proposition that all men are created equal. Now we are engaged in a great civil war, testing whether that nation, or any nation so conceived, and so dedicated can long endure." Because the Gettysburg Address is considered Lincoln's clearest intention to link the emancipation of slaves to his original war aim of preserving the union and because it is considered the greatest speech in American history, Lincoln's eloquent words should be quoted directly.

Second, students should consider the length of the quotation. They should use only those parts that are absolutely necessary to prove their point. The integration of quotation fragments into a student essay rather than the use of block quotations is preferred because it demonstrates the student's understanding of the quote and how that particular piece of evidence supports his argument. For example, when the noted black abolitionist and orator Frederick Douglass was accused, along with other radical abolitionists, of precipitating the Civil War, he responded in the following way:

> The abolitionists of this country have been charged with bringing on the war between the North and South, and in one sense this is true. Had there been no antislavery agitation in the North, there would have been no active antislavery anywhere to resist the demands of the Slave Power at the South, and where there is no resistance there can be no war. Slavery would then have been nationalized, and the whole country would then have been subjected to its power. Resistance to slavery and the extension of slavery invited and provoked secession and war to perpetuate and extend the slave system.[1]

The same statement can be delivered more effectively in the following manner:

> When radical abolitionists were accused of starting the Civil War, Frederick Douglass, a famous black abolitionist, admitted that the charge was partly "true" and that if there "had been no antislavery agitation in the North" slavery would have been spread throughout the "whole country."

Finally, students must be told that a failure to acknowledge the findings of another person, conflicting information (e.g., differing interpretations of a topic, dates, or statistics), ideas that can be traced to another historian, or direct quotation of another person is literary theft, or plagiarism. When plagiarism occurs, it is treated as a major offense against the standards of academic honesty. Punishment can range from redoing the paper to a failing grade, depending upon the severity of the offense. Deliberate plagiarism, especially at the middle school level, is relatively rare. Most of what appears to be plagiarism in student work is unintentional borrowing, a result of inexperience, of carelessness in note taking, and of uncertainty as to the degree of documentation expected. The general rule for students is If in doubt, footnote!

Some teachers may believe that these points are too complicated for middle schoolers to understand—not so! Taking note cards is a common practice at the middle school level for such things as oral reports, research for portable exhibits, models of historical sites, and simulation exercises. Having students take the practice to the next level by writing a paper is not too much to ask at this age level. What they do need is careful guidance from the teacher. Besides, if the students work in groups, the paper writing will, no doubt, be completed by those students who have a natural interest or motivation in writing and will learn these skills quickly.

For taking notes I instruct students to place a heading on each three-by-five-inch note card with an indicator for book (B), primary source document (D), article (A), or interview (I) in the upper right-hand corner. Since they should already have a bibliography, which includes author, title, and all other relevant information about the sources being used, they need only to distinguish one book or article from another (i.e., A1, A2, A3 for articles and B1, B2, B3 for books). I ask students to take only one note on each card so the outlining and writing process will go more smoothly. Time spent carefully taking notes saves time in the later stages of writing. For example, say a student quotes or paraphrases sixteen separate times from the same source and places all of these references on three cards. When settling down to write the paper, she won't want to use this information in the same order, or even consecutively. If each idea is placed on a separate card, on the other hand, the student can organize the information more effectively when constructing the outline and the paper. Students should also avoid abbreviations when note taking. Abbreviations often result in confusion. Finally, each note card should have a subject label, or a brief descriptive phrase that indicates the heading and subheading for each note. The cards should match the outline and be used with the outline to write the paper. Again, this method will save time and limit frustration when the student is completing the outline. Students then hand in their notes and outlines to the teacher for feedback and/or grade. There is an outline for a paper on the Quaker stationmaster Thomas Garrett on the following page.

Thomas Garrett of Wilmington

I. Introduction

    A: Harriet Tubman goes to Thomas Garrett for money

    B: Thesis: Thomas Garrett was one of the most important station-masters on the Underground Railroad. He worked together with other white and black abolitionists to free hundreds of slaves.

II. Body Sections

    A: Historical background on Thomas Garrett

        1. Born on August 21, 1789 in Upper Darby, Pennsylvania

        2. He was raised as a Quaker

            a. Quaker belief in equality

            b. God's law vs. Fugitive Slave law

        3. Photo analysis of Thomas Garrett

        4. Garrett's marriages

            a. To Mary Sharpless on October 14, 1813 at the Birmingham Meeting House in Chester County. They had five children: Sarah, Anna, Henry, Margaret, and Elwood.

            b. To Rachel Mendenhall. They had one son, Eli.

    B: Garrett's Underground Railroad activities

        1. 1813—kidnapping of family's paid servant inspires him

        2. 1820s—moves to Wilmington, Delaware, where he becomes a stationmaster

            a. story of slave owner who threatens to shoot Garrett

            b. story of how he disguised runaways

        3. 1848—Garrett tried and found guilty of hiding fugitive slaves.

    C: Work with black abolitionists

        1. William Still

        2. Harriet Tubman

        3. Comegys Munson

        4. Severn Johnson

        5. Harry Craig

III. Conclusion

    A: Garrett dies on January 25, 1871

    B: What we learned from Garrett

This is a fairly detailed outline, which, no doubt, began as a more vague, working outline. The outline evolves in a natural progression that allows the students to prove the thesis. The first body section addresses historical context, showing Garrett's motives for becoming an abolitionist. The second body section develops those involvements as they apply to the Underground Railroad. Body section 3 caps the argument by showing that Garrett did, in fact, work with black agents on the secret route to freedom. Finally, the conclusion intends to tell the reader what contemporary lesson the students learned from their research.

The purpose of keeping such an outline is to allow the students to think through the factual material they've gathered and the mechanics of the paper before they actually begin to write. The act of organizing this information is extremely important because it gives the students a tangible product of their work.

Assessment of Two Research Papers

Now let's examine each part of the outline as it has been developed in the final paper itself and do so with an eye on certain strategies teachers can use to aid students through the writing process. This particular paper was completed by a group of three students who divided the research and writing chores. One student served as the editor of the final paper to ensure the fluidity of the writing. It's important to remember that all endnotes immediately following the various sections are the students'—not mine!

> **Introduction:** Once, when Harriet Tubman asked Thomas Garrett for $23 to help her conduct a small band of runaway slaves to freedom, the Quaker stationmaster replied: "I am not a wealthy man, but I will give thee what I can."
>
> "You have $23 for me though," insisted Tubman.
>
> "How does thee know that?" he asked.
>
> Without a second thought, the black conductor simply said: "God told me." Garrett soon handed her $24 and some odd cents.[1]
>
> Thomas Garrett was one of the most important stationmasters on the Underground Railroad. He worked together with other white and black abolitionists to free several hundred slaves.
>
> **Endnote:**
>
> 1. Sarah Bradford, *Harriet Tubman: The Moses of Her People (1886)* (reprinted by Applewood Books, Bedford, MA, 1993), 86.

The introduction opens with an exchange between Thomas Garrett and Harriet Tubman. This is a creative way to begin the paper as it captures the reader's attention and, in terms of the argument, illustrates the close-knit nature of the relationship between these two agents. It also identifies Garrett as a white stationmaster and Tubman as a "black conductor," suggesting the interracial cooperation upon which their efforts were based. This brief narrative sets the stage nicely for the thesis statement that Garrett was "one of the most important stationmasters on the Underground Railroad" and that "he worked together with other white and black abolitionists to free several hundred slaves."

Establishing a clear thesis statement early on is important. While the thesis statement of this particular paper would not be acceptable at the high school level, where a thesis must be a more objective statement, it is sufficient for a middle school paper, which is basically informative rather than argumentative. Still, middle school students, who tend to write narrative chronologies because of their attraction to storytelling, can and should be introduced to thematically organized essays aimed at proving a particular argument.

Encourage students to think about the main point they hope to deliver to readers in their "story." Do they want to focus on the dangers of being an Underground Railroad agent? The courage of the stationmaster? Cooperation between races? The advantage of working in a group is that the students can brainstorm with each other. Thinking aloud can be a very constructive method for organizing the themes of a paper. Another strategy that is helpful is to challenge students to determine the main point, or thesis, by having them do an improvisational skit on the Underground Railroad agent or site. Acting speaks louder than words. Middle schoolers often become intellectually inspired through physical engagement, and, if nothing else, the process of acting out their ideas can often get students to externalize those ideas on paper.

As you read the various body sections of the student work that follows, you will see the tendency to tell a story within each one. At the same time, however, the students have done a fairly good job of organizing the paper by theme. Body section 1 addresses Garrett's personal background:

Body Section 1: Born on August 21, 1789 in Upper Darby, Pennsylvania, Garrett was raised as a Quaker.[2] The Quakers believed that slaves were spiritually equal, but most were uncomfortable violating the Fugitive Slave Law, which required all citizens to assist in the recapture of runaways.[3] Garrett believed that God's law was more important than the civil law and became an active agent on the Underground Railroad. His involvement began in 1813, when a free black woman who worked for his parents was kidnapped from their farm. She was a well-loved member of the family and Thomas wanted her back. He saddled his horse and raced after the kidnapper, following his wagon trail. When he caught up with him, Garrett demanded and was given the servant. This was the turning point in his career. When he realized the plight of African-Americans, he had to do something about it.[4]

The photograph of Garrett [Figure 4–1] was taken sometime around 1850, when he would have been 61 years old. He has a pot belly that you can see beneath his vest and looks very serious, like a man determined to fight for his beliefs. He is dressed in a suit and bow-tie, which shows that he was a person with some wealth and had the money to help runaways.[5]

Figure 4–1. *Thomas Garrett, age 61*

Garrett was married twice in his lifetime. On October 14, 1813, he married Mary Sharpless at the Birmingham Meeting House in Chester County. Together they had five children: Sarah, Anna, Henry, Margaret, and Elwood.[6] After she died, on July 13, 1828, he married again. His second wife was Rachel Mendenhall. They had one son, Eli.[7]

Endnotes:

2. James A. McGowan, *Station Master of the Underground Railroad: The Life and Letters of Thomas Garrett.* (Moylan, PA: The Whimsie Press, 1977), 17.

3. Charles Blockson, "The Underground Railroad: The Quaker Connection," *For Emancipation & Education: Some Black & Quaker Efforts,* edited by Eliza Cope Harrison. (Philadelphia: Germantown Historical Society, 1997), 36–43.

4. McGowan, *Station Master,* 25–26.

5. Photograph of Thomas Garrett in old age (ca. 1850), Photo Archives, Chester County Historical Society, West Chester, Pennsylvania.

6. McGowan, *Station Master,* 28–29.

7. Ibid., 43.

The first body section gives the reader historical context as well as an understanding of Garrett's Quaker beliefs and how they influenced his decision to violate the Fugitive Slave Law of 1850. The mention of the Fugitive Slave Law as well as the dates of Garrett's marriages are important to set the time period for the events discussed in the essay. Garrett was, in other words, a product of the early to mid-nineteenth century, when the institution of slavery was a major concern in the United States. The fact that his Quaker faith, with its belief in the spiritual equality of all human beings, condemned the institution of slavery serves to explain the tendency to oppose that institution. The issue of motive is extremely important for students to understand when assessing the lives of those who became Underground Railroad agents. Accordingly, the observation that Garrett chose "God's law," based on his understanding of the "spiritual equality" of all human beings, over civil law in assisting runaway slaves is an especially important insight.

The students then demonstrate how Garrett acted on this belief in his rescue of a family servant who was kidnapped by a slave catcher. James McGowan, Garrett's biographer, believes that this incident was a "mystical revelation that profoundly influenced the course of his life," a kind of epiphany that set the stage for his future as a stationmaster on the Underground Railroad.[2] Note that the students decided to deviate from their outline in telling this story. The 1813 kidnapping, according to the outline, was intended to be part of body section 2, which addresses Garrett's Underground Railroad activities. But for whatever reason, the students decided to place the story in the first body section. Considering the middle school penchant for stories and the fact that every section of the outline except for the first body section contained a story, it's possible that the students made this decision for the sake of balance, that is, to include at least one engaging story in each body section. The teacher might want to point out the discrepancy between the outline and the final essay as an example that outlines are really loose guidelines to follow as the essay is being crafted. Writing is a constant process of thinking and rethinking and there is nothing wrong with deviating from the outline, especially if it results in a stronger final product.

The photo offers further confirmation of Garrett's commitment to assisting fugitive slaves. The students explain that Garrett, by nature, was a man who was not only "determined to fight for his beliefs" but also "had the money to help runaways." The photo serves as one of two primary sources used in the paper and demonstrates the critical thinking skills of these three students. The paper also relies heavily on McGowan's biography of Garrett, which is understandable since it is the only major secondary source on this Underground Railroad agent.

Now let's look at the second body section.

Body Section 2: In the 1820s, Garrett moved to Wilmington, Delaware, where he made his living as an iron merchant and also became one of the most active agents on the Underground Railroad. A hearty, humorous, resourceful, and most of all fearless man, Garrett didn't know the meaning of fear. Once, an angry slave owner told the Quaker abolitionist that if he ever came South, he would shoot him. "Well," said Garrett, "I am thinking of going that way before long and I will call upon thee." Shortly after, Garrett was traveling in the South on business and called on the man. "How does thee do, friend?" said the Wilmington stationmaster. "Here I am, thee can shoot me if thee likes." But being confronted face-to-face with him, the slave owner backed down. [8]

Garrett never tried to hide the fact that he was helping fugitive slaves escape, but ended up making great sacrifices in order to assist in daring escapes. Once he was hiding a female fugitive and his house was being watched by slave catchers. In order to escape, Garrett disguised the fugitive as his wife with a large scoop bonnet that completely covered her face. Once out the door, he boarded his dearborn wagon with the runaway and rode safely to the next station.[9]

In another instance, Garrett disguised a fugitive as a farm worker. When he learned that the fugitive had been caught and taken to the magistrate's office, Garrett secured his release by leading the judge to believe that the fugitive was actually his employee. Remarkably he never lied in giving this explanation.[10]

In 1848 Garrett was charged with and found guilty of hiding fugitive slaves. Being heavily fined by the Delaware court and warned "not to meddle with slaves again," he told the federal marshal: "I now consider the penalty imposed upon me as a license for the remainder of my life." Turning to the courtroom spectators, he added: "If any of you know of any slave who needs assistance, send him to me, as I now publicly pledge myself to double my diligence to assist slaves in obtaining their freedom."[11]

The $5,000 fine almost bankrupted Garrett, but Patrick Holland, a working-class Irishman who assisted the Wilmington stationmaster in conducting fugitives to freedom, offered to help him. Holland offered him a few hundred dollars, saying: "Take it, Mr. Garrett and go into business again; if you are successful, you will pay me again; if not, I am yet young and can earn more."[12]

Endnotes:

8. Judith Bentley, *"Dear Friend": Thomas Garrett & William Still, Collaborators on the Underground Railroad.* (New York: Dutton, 1997), 20.

9. Terence Maguire, "Slavery, Freedom, and the Underground Railroad," *"Desperate River," Quiet Creek.* (Unpublished Manuscript, 1990), 130–31.

10. Ibid.

11. McGowan, *Station Master,* 65–66.

12. *Wilmington (DE) Daily Commercial:* August ? 1877.

Body section 2 begins with the topic sentence "In the 1820s, Garrett moved to Wilmington, Delaware, where he made his living as an iron merchant and also became one of the most active agents on the Underground Railroad." The topic sentence signals to the reader that the paper is turning to a new subject: Garrett's activities as "one of the most active agents on the Underground Railroad." The students prove this point through four anecdotes concerning those activities: (1) confronting a slave owner; (2) disguising a female fugitive to help her escape; (3) fooling a local magistrate into believing that a male fugitive was actually an employee of his; and (4) the 1848 trial. All of these anecdotes reinforce the students' earlier insights about Garrett's strong abolitionist beliefs and his determination to end slavery, even if it meant breaking the civil law.

Of the four anecdotes, however, Garrett's 1848 trial is the best documented, because it was written about in a contemporary newspaper. All the other anecdotes come from secondary sources. While there is nothing wrong with relying on secondary source material for a research paper of this nature, books written long after the actual events often raise the question of credibility. If students are being given the opportunity to do a rewrite (because there was a lack of primary sources used), the teacher might want to register the difference between primary and secondary information by having students play a game like Whisper Down the Lane. In this game eight to ten students stand next to each other in a line. The first student whispers into the ear of the second student a factual statement about the Underground Railroad agent being investigated. The second student embellishes the statement with information that cannot be proven and whispers it to the third student. Each time the information is "whispered down the lane," it is further embellished. Finally, the last student reveals the heavily embellished statement and compares it with the original one. This exercise is a fun way to show students that factual information, or primary source material, can often become distorted in its retelling by others. The retelling is actually hearsay, or secondary source material that is not always reliable.

In the case of the group essay we have been studying, the anecdotes about Garrett have credibility because his identification as a stationmaster is heavily documented through contemporary letters. But what if Garrett weren't a credible figure?

Students, when confronted with this problem, are forced to do careful genealogical research to substantiate the individual's Underground Railroad involvement. Some of the questions they should ask are

1. How likely is it that the anecdote was an eyewitness account?

2. Are there any descendants who can verify the anecdote?

3. How consistent are the versions of the anecdote as reported in various sources?

The main point in identifying the validity of any Underground Railroad legend, or a site for that matter, is to establish the individual associated with it as, in fact, an agent. This is done best through primary source documentation and secondly through oral tradition based upon family history and/or genealogy.[3]

Now we will consider the third body section.

Body Section 3: Thomas Garrett realized that he needed help from the local black community if he was to be successful in guiding fugitives to freedom. Among his closest friends was William Still, a free black man who was also a Philadelphia stationmaster. The two men wrote letters back and forth communicating about the runaways they were passing between them. When Garrett received fugitives, he knew he could send them to Philadelphia to seek help from Still because of the black abolitionist's many contacts in New York, New England and Canada.[12] There were other free black people who helped Garrett as well.

Harriet Tubman, considered the most famous conductor on the Underground Railroad, was a frequent visitor to Garrett's Wilmington station. He often provided her with food, clothing and money in order to guide her runaways on to the North.[13] Garrett also hired local black men to conduct runaways over the Mason-Dixon line and into Chester County. Among them were Comegys Munson, Severn Johnson, Harry Craig and Joseph Walker, who sometimes rowed runaways across the Christina River in their journey to freedom.[14] Together with these conductors, Garrett is believed to have helped more than 2,000 slaves to freedom.[15]

Endnotes:

12. Bentley, *Dear Friend*, 36–57.

13. McGowan, *Station Master*, 89–90.

14. Maguire, "Slavery, Freedom, and the Underground Railroad," 134.

15. Thomas Garrett to Samuel May Jr., 11 month, 24, 1863, Friends Historical Library, Swarthmore College.

Body section 3 addresses the third theme of the essay—the biracial nature of Garrett's activities—and offers the final proof of the thesis. While the students do a nice job of identifying the black agents with whom Garrett worked, they only summarize the interaction between these agents and Garrett. A more effective proof would have quoted from Garrett's letters to William Still or offered another anecdote about Harriet Tubman's many visits to Garrett's station at Wilmington. Nevertheless, the students do offer some relatively unknown information in identifying four other, lesser-known black agents—Comegys Munson, Severn Johnson, Harry Craig, and Joseph Walker—and the nature of their activities on the Underground Railroad. Just as important, this little-known information comes from a primary source, Garrett's November 24, 1863, letter to Samuel May Jr., a copy of which is located at the Friends Historical Library at Swarthmore College.

Finally, let's look at the paper's conclusion.

Conclusion: Only a few days before his death on January 25, 1871, Thomas said, "I now must own up that I am an old man. While I have been favored to be cheerful, my work here on this earth is nearly done."[16] He is buried in the graveyard of the Wilmington Meeting House at Fourth and West Streets.

Thomas Garrett's example inspires us to work together to solve the problems of race discrimination in our country, no matter if we're black or white.

Endnote:

16. McGowan, *Station Master*, 81.

The conclusion sums up Garrett's Underground Railroad activities by using his own epitaph. This is an especially creative way to end the paper for three reasons: (1) it summarizes the paper, which is what a conclusion is supposed to do; (2) it allows Garrett to speak for himself about his own understanding of his antislavery contributions; and (3) it offers solid proof since the quote is taken from a primary source document.

Although I would like to have read a more detailed comment about what the students learned from their research and writing of the paper and how that lesson could be applied to race relations today, the statement on the importance of biracial cooperation is a valuable one for all of us to aspire to. If the students learned that lesson through this research project, then it was an unequivocal success.

Many middle school students like to complete their papers on Underground Railroad agents because of their interest in the personalities of the movement. To be sure, some knowledge of the agent is necessary even when researching a site. Chances are better that documentary evidence exists for an agent than for a site.

Oral tradition is often the basis for identifying a site as an Underground Railroad station. Too often the oral history is spun from more than 150 years of folklore and mythology designed to boost the pride of a small-town community.[4] Worse, it may come from the local real estate agent who claims that the antebellum-era house for sale was once a stop on the Underground Railroad in order to add a certain allure to the house as well as to guarantee a commission. Nevertheless, there is value in researching an Underground Railroad station, whether it's real or imagined. Let's take a look at a middle school paper that investigated such a site: the Honeycomb African Methodist Episcopal Church in Lima, Pennsylvania.

> **Introduction:** "Honeycomb"? Isn't that a cereal? Or something found in a bee hive?
>
> Not in this case.
>
> "Honeycomb" is the name of a Union African Methodist Episcopal church that served as an important station on the invisible passage to freedom called the Underground Railroad.

Although this introduction is not as developed as the one in the previous paper, the middle school sense of humor is apparent and offers a clever way to introduce the subject, especially when there is not a lot of information known about the site. The three students who worked on this paper are aiming to prove that Honeycomb was, in fact, an Underground Railroad station. Thus, a statement of that proof becomes the thesis itself. This attempt to kill two birds with one stone is completely acceptable in a paper of this nature, where the evidence offered, as descriptive as it may be, is designed to prove the credibility of the site. An alternative approach would be to begin the essay with one of the irrefutable Underground Railroad facts that are given in the essay itself. This might be the identification of a known stationmaster who belonged to the church or a documented rescue that took place among the parishioners. The main idea, or thesis, would be the religious inspiration of Honeycomb in the Underground Railroad activities of its members.

Body Section 1: During the middle of the nineteenth century, a group of nine black citizens in Lima, a section of Middletown in Delaware County, wanted to attend church services, but the nearest church was a Quaker church in Springfield. Since this was a rather far distance to travel, either on foot or by horse and buggy, the group agreed to begin their own church in Middletown.

At first they took turns meeting in each other's homes. As their numbers grew, they considered building a real church. The problem was that blacks could not purchase land or own property. But even if there was a way to own land, what land was the right place to build a church?

The first problem was solved when a white lawyer bought land for the black worshippers. While they were able to build their church on the property, the lawyer continued to own the land. The second problem was solved when one of the founders, James White, had a dream of sheep grazing and interpreted his dream to mean that the new church should be built near a place where sheep graze. A sheep farm was found, and land for the church was acquired on February 2, 1852 from Mary Garnett for a sum of $12.00. [1]

In 1852 ground was broken for the new church. A porous rock, nicknamed honeycomb rock, was used in building the church. Thus, the nickname of the church became Honeycomb Church, which eventually became its real name. The church is formally known as the Union African Methodist Episcopal Honeycomb Church. The founding members were: James White, Mary White, Rachel Brown, William Sadler, Ester Sadler, Cornellus Barnes, Margaret Brown, and Hannah Ballard. [2]

Members of the church were happy to finally have their own place of worship, with Luke Smith agreeing to serve as the first pastor. But the church had no running water or pump. The floors were of bare wood, and seats were long, narrow benches with no backs. There was only one outhouse for the entire congregation. [3]

Despite all of these inconveniences, the church became the center of black social life in Middletown. Dances, parties, socials, meetings, and church events, such as weddings and funerals, brought the community together frequently. All music at the church was vocal with clapping. Songs were in "common meter," with congregants making them up according to how they felt. The music had no beat, but was poetic in nature. It began by someone making up a verse and singing it. This was followed by someone else who added a line that they made up. Whoever wanted to sing and add another verse could, as long as the verses rhymed.[4] Often songs were heard in the woods surrounding the church, the most popular site for camp meetings. Held each summer, the camp meetings sometimes lasted as long as two weeks.

Soon the church was known throughout the county. People came by foot from as far as Gradyville. Those who lived in Avondale caught a train and walked from Elwyn Station to Honeycomb.[5]

Endnotes:

1. Loretta Rodgers, "The Trackless Train," *Delaware County Sunday Times*: February 28, 1999.

2. Henry S. Pearson, *Middletown Township, Delaware County, Pennsylvania*. (Media: Baker Printing, 1985), 162.

3. Ibid., 163.

4. Pearson, *Middletown Township*, 162.

5. Interview of Anna Moat, Historian, Honeycomb U.A.M.E. Church: February 10, 2001.

Body section 1 relates the origins and historical context of the church. Like many African American churches, Honeycomb was founded as a place of worship by a small group of black residents in a predominantly white community. As the students point out, the church quickly became a "center of black social life" where "dances, parties, socials, meetings . . . weddings and funerals" frequently took place. Its origins were inspired by the need for self-help and community building. The students' observation is confirmed by historians who have already identified similar patterns in other free black communities in the antebellum North. Because of the common bonds of kinship and, perhaps for some, the experience of slavery itself, these free blacks felt more acutely the need to aid runaway slaves in their quest for freedom than the white abolitionists in their local community.[5]

Body Section 2: Because the church was active during a time period when the South practiced slavery, many of its members were former slaves who had a strong desire to help their black brothers and sisters who were still in bondage. As the Underground Railroad developed throughout the land, Honeycomb Church was sometimes used as a stop on the passage to freedom. Peter Spencer, an A.M.E. minister whose church was located on Route 13 in the state of Delaware, sent runaways through the woods and creeks to the small church. From Honeycomb, the fugitives traveled on to Canada. Some runaway slaves came to Sunday services or midweek prayer meetings. Afterwards, they blended in with the members of the congregation and left with those families who offered to provide them with shelter.[6]

Blending into a black community was easier than being among whites, but there was still the danger of being caught and returned to the slave masters.[7] Some of the songs sung by the congregation were used as codes for runaways, and contained secret messages that could be interpreted by the listeners. Honeycomb Church used these kinds of coded songs to help runaways on their journey to freedom.[8] Hiding places, for emergency situations, were available in the ceiling of the church or under the floor. According to oral history, runaway slaves were hidden in a crawl space above the church's tin ceiling.[9] There are also stories of runaways who passed through the church. Among the most popular of these stories is that of William Spradley.

Spradley, a confederate spy, who was still considered "property" by his southern bosses, walked off with two other slaves to scout an area. Instead of returning, they hooked up with the Underground Railroad and found themselves at the Honeycomb Church. They stayed there until nightfall, when they were moved to the Pennell farm nearby. Two of the runaways continued on to freedom, but Spradley stayed behind. For a number of years he worked at the Pennell Farm where Pennell's daughter taught him to read and write. Eventually he became a member of the congregation and fell in love with a local girl. He married her in 1869, the year the church received its charter. He was a faithful church member and performed the duties of church secretary for sixty years.[10]

Endnotes:

6. Garcia-Barrio, Constance. "Underground Railroad Stations: Reminders of Perilous Journeys," *Philadelphia Inquirer.* February 4, 1991.

7. Charles L. Blockson, *The Underground Railroad in Pennsylvania* (Jacksonville, FL: Flame International, 1981), 64.

8. Rodgers, "The Trackless Train."

9. Ibid.

10. Robert F. O'Neill, "Underground Railroad and Delco Church Were on the Same Tracks," *Philadelphia Inquirer.* February 9, 2001.

Body section 2 establishes the connection between Honeycomb and the Underground Railroad. The students tell us that Peter Spencer, a noted African Methodist Episcopal minister from Delaware "sent runaways through the woods and creeks to the small church" and that "from Honeycomb, the fugitives traveled on to Canada." We are also told that "some runaway slaves came to Sunday services or midweek prayer meetings" and "blended in with the members of the congregation" who, in turn, "offered to provide them with shelter." The fact that this information comes from secondary source material—books, present-day newspaper accounts, and an interview—is not unusual for papers that focus on Underground Railroad sites. Because of the illegal nature of the movement, very little primary source documentation exists to substantiate connections between a specific site and the Underground Railroad unless it comes directly from an agent himself. And few agents took the risk of recording their activities because of the possibility of incriminating themselves if their writings were discovered by the civil authorities. To complicate matters, many stationmasters moved to a different location after a period of years, probably to eliminate suspicion of their clandestine activities. In the case of Honeycomb Church, primary source documentation is especially difficult to find because the free blacks who belonged to the church relied on folklore and the oral tradition to tell their history.

The students who wrote this paper acknowledge their reliance on folklore with the observation that the congregants "used . . . coded songs to help runaways on their journey to freedom." The students also relied on oral history accounts, which reveal that "runaway slaves were hidden in a crawl space above the church's tin ceiling." The person who popularized these stories is William Spradley, a slave-turned-Confederate-spy, "who hooked up with the Underground Railroad . . . at Honeycomb" and eventually became "a faithful church member."

Because folklore and oral tradition are so intimately connected with the Underground Railroad, teachers might want to register the importance of these traditions in students' own lives. Have students recall some of the family anecdotes, legends, or amusing stories that are told around the holiday table. These kinds of stories are especially popular among families whose ancestors immigrated to the United States after the Civil War. Often, they are humorous recollections involving the naïveté of an ancestor who was trying to navigate the customs and conventions of a new American society, which were so foreign to those of his native land. It was not really very different for runaways, who not only had to navigate the perilous journey to freedom but also had to learn an entirely different way of life than the one they had known in bondage.

Conclusion: Honeycomb Church witnessed several changes since it was first constructed from honeycomb rock, including the building of a new frame structure and the enlargement of the facility to include a basement, choir room, a pastor's study, new pews, a new and larger parking lot, a kitchen, and stained glass windows and doors. Besides the physical changes, Honeycomb Church is still remembered for its vital role in helping runaway slaves escape to freedom.

Although this conclusion updates the reader on the physical improvements to the church over time, it doesn't do a very good job of summarizing the main points of the paper. Nor does it tell us what lessons the students learned from their research that might be useful in addressing the issue of race relations today. Nevertheless, the paper—through the use of folklore and oral tradition—does give credibility to Honeycomb Church as a stop on the Underground Railroad.

Summary

The process of researching and writing a local history paper on the Underground Railroad develops quite naturally from the earlier documentary and photographic analyses discussed in Chapters 2 and 3. It's also a wonderful way to integrate the skills of thinking, reading, and writing in a critical fashion with the subject of the Underground Railroad. Some teachers may think that this kind of project is too complicated for middle school students. But I have found that when middle schoolers are challenged, they often respond with their best work, especially when they have a natural interest in the topic. The Underground Railroad, with its stories of daring escapes and courageous rescues, piques the curiosity and imaginations of middle school students. Offering them the opportunity to learn about the history and operation of the movement by actually exploring it firsthand can only make for a more engaging experience with the subject.

Endnotes

1. Frederick Douglass, *Life and Times of Frederick Douglass* (New York, 1882), 607.

2. James A. McGowan, *Station Master on the Underground Railroad: The Life and Letters of Thomas Garrett* (Moylan, PA: Whimsie, 1977), 26.

3. See Oloye Adeyemon, "Researching the Legends of People, Incidents, Sites and Routes of the Underground Railroad," *Network to Freedom* (official newsletter of the National Park Service's National Underground Railroad Network to Freedom), (March 2003): 1–4.

4. See Larry Gara, *The Liberty Line: The Legend of the Underground Railroad* (Lexington: University of Kentucky, 1961) for the mythology surrounding Underground Railroad sites. For information on how to determine the credibility of an alleged site, see National Register, History and Education, National Park Service, *Exploring a Common Past: Researching and Interpreting the Underground Railroad* (Washington, DC: U.S. Government Printing Office, 1998); National Register, History and Education, National Park Service, *Underground Railroad Resources in the United States: Theme Study* (Washington, DC: U.S. Government Printing Office, 2000); and John Beck, "Revealing the Facts: Practical Advice on Interpreting Myths

at Your Historic Site," *Network to Freedom* (newsletter of the National Park Service's National Underground Railroad Network to Freedom) (March 2003): 1–2.

5. James Oliver Horton, *Free People of Color: Inside the African American Community* (Washington, DC: Smithsonian Institution Press, 1993); James Oliver Horton and Lois E. Horton, *In Hope of Liberty: Culture, Community and Protest Among Northern Free Blacks, 1700–1860* (New York: Oxford University Press, 1997); and Julie Winch, *Philadelphia's Black Elite: Activism, Accommodation, and the Struggle for Autonomy, 1787–1848* (Philadelphia: Temple University Press, 1988).

Chapter Five

Personalizing the Railroad
In-Class Activities

One of the reasons the Underground Railroad fascinates youngsters is because of the covert manner in which participants communicated with each other. The vocabulary of the railroad was a superficial cover for the clandestine purpose of transporting slaves to freedom in the North. Secrecy was necessary, of course, because of the illegal nature of the movement. Middle school students, in particular, love to keep their own secrets, or at least share them only within a close circle of friends. They revel in the ability to operate on a higher, more abstract plane of communication with each other, as it offers a special kind of control over their environment. Middle schoolers are also in the process of establishing personal identities. Although they are no longer children, preadolescents have not yet reached adulthood either because of financial and psychological dependence on parents. It is in this middle ground between childhood and adulthood that secrecy is often associated with "personal intimacy," "privacy," and even "rebellion."[1] But secrecy is only part of the appeal of the Underground Railroad.

Personal relevance is just as strong a motivator. Youngsters gravitate to the Underground Railroad because of its human element and their ability to relate with emotions like pain, sorrow, and desperation. They tend to feel more acutely than adults such feelings because of the rapid physiological, psychological, and emotional changes that are taking place in their young lives, especially during preadolescence.[2] They want to hear about the personal sacrifices, struggles, and rewards of people who lived in the past. They also want to understand how, if at all, those sacrifices, struggles, and rewards influenced their own lives.

After one of my living history portrayals of Quaker stationmaster Thomas Garrett, a middle school student asked, "So what? Why should we care about Garrett and his helping two thousand slaves to freedom? Why don't you tell us about what happened to the Underground Railroad today?"

100

The question was an impressive one because it cut to the heart of why we have invested so much time researching, writing, and teaching students about the Underground Railroad, and that is because of the spirit of interracial cooperation that informed the movement and how our contemporary society can benefit from that spirit of cooperation. We, too, wonder where the Underground Railroad is today, though not in the same way that the curious middle schooler did. We are much less concerned about the specific location of existing stations and the idiosyncratic hiding places that can be found inside them than we're interested in encouraging students to pursue that same spirit of interracial cooperation so that our society can bridge the racial divide that still exists today. Studying the Underground Railroad can be an important entry point into class discussions about cultural similarities and differences between African Americans and white Americans as well as between those two social groups and others, like Asian Americans and Hispanic Americans. Some teachers may want to integrate community service into the study of the Underground Railroad by having students from different schools in their district collaborate on the research for a local Underground Railroad site. The act of brainstorming, discussing, and researching such a topic among groups of different social and economic backgrounds creates the kind of multicultural cooperation upon which the success of the Underground Railroad depended.

Whether we teach in schools or history museums, educators have an awesome responsibility to cultivate good citizenship and social awareness among youngsters. One of the most effective ways to teach those principles is through cooperative learning. The exercises that follow emphasize a living history classroom, or how to teach the Underground Railroad in a fun way that engages both teachers and students. The exercises were created to develop listening, critical thinking, and empathy building.

A Critical Thinking Exercise

Historians have tried to estimate the number of people who escaped from slavery to freedom. Figure 5–1 will give your students a good idea of how many escaped and how many remained in bondage by 1860. Each circle represents one hundred thousand slaves. Each line contains ten circles, and there are four lines. Ask students to calculate how many slaves there were in 1860 by completing the following equations:

100,000 slaves × 10 circles = 1,000,000 slaves
1,000,000 slaves × 4 lines = 4,000,000 slaves total

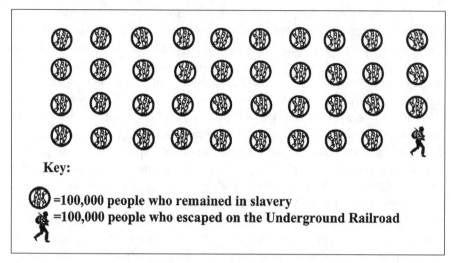

Figure 5–1. *How many slaves escaped on the Underground Railroad?*

Circles represent those who remained in slavery. The figure of a fugitive represents the most liberal estimate of the number of slaves who escaped on the Underground Railroad. Of the four million enslaved people, how many escaped using the Underground Railroad? The answer is one hundred thousand people. At best, only one in forty enslaved people escaped on the Underground Railroad. Ask students why they think the number was so small. Some considerations may include strict control over every aspect of slave life; harsh punishment for those who tried to escape and were caught; and the fact that owners made sure that slaves were powerless by limiting their possessions and preventing their education.

Ask students if they would try to escape if they were slaves in the nineteenth century. Remind them that their decision to stay or leave might depend upon their life circumstances. Divide students into small groups and have them consider the reasons to stay and reasons to leave in the following list. After the students have had an opportunity to discuss these reasons, ask a representative from each group to explain their life circumstances from the list and whether each would be a reason to leave or a reason to stay. There are no correct or incorrect answers. Instead, the purpose of the exercise is to encourage students to think about decision making and the human condition.

1. Your master is sick and will probably die soon.
2. You can't read.
3. You live fifteen miles from a free state.
4. You've heard rumors that your family will soon be sold.

5. You have learned to read.

6. You've heard that Quakers will help runaways.

7. It's summer.

8. Your husband/wife is free, living in Canada.

9. You are forty-five years old.

10. Your master mistreats you.

11. You've seen a captured runaway beaten with a bullwhip.

12. You don't know which way to run.

13. You've already been caught trying to escape once.

14. Your cousin was just sold to the Deep South for attempting an escape.

15. You are a servant in the master's house and treated better than field slaves.

16. You live 350 miles from a free state.

17. Your grandmother is old and frail.

18. Your master has always treated you kindly.

19. You are only ten years old.

20. There is a new baby in your family.

21. You have a large family, all at the same plantation.

22. You have no living relatives.

23. It's winter.

24. You are twenty-one years old.

More motivated students may want to reconsider some of their responses by reading the following primary source quotes:

> I have observed this in my experience of slavery: that whenever my condition was improved, instead of its increasing my contentment, it only increased my desire to be free, and set me to thinking of plans to gain my freedom.
>
> —*Frederick Douglass*[3]

For conditions 4, 8, and 21:

> I was free but there was no one to welcome me to freedom. I was a stranger in a strange land. To this solemn resolution I came: I was free and my parents, brothers and sisters should be free also; I would make a home for them in the North, and the Lord helping me, I would bring them all there. "Oh, dear Lord," I said, "I ain't got no friend but you. Come to my help, Lord, for I'm in trouble!"
>
> —*Harriet Tubman*[4]

For conditions 19, 20, and 22:

Ole Marse John ain't never had no chillun by his wife, so Marsa was always goin' down to the [slave] shacks to visit Martha. Marsa John used to treat Martha's boy, Jim, jus' like his own son, which he was. Him used to run all over de big house.

—Henry Ferry, a Virginian slave[5]

For conditions 2, 4, 10, and 11:

I was raised in a city in Maryland, and was a slave from birth until twenty years of age. The slaves in cities are better treated than those on farms and plantations. When I was young, I was sent to school for white children. When I was about ten years old, my first master died. My mistress married again. My new master wished to hire me out on a farm, but the mistress did not give her consent and I remained in the city.

—John A. Hunter, a Maryland slave[6]

Decoding Slave Songs

Underground Railroad activities were secret because they were illegal. Escaping slaves who were caught would be returned to bondage and could be severely punished or sold to the Deep South, where living and working conditions tended to be horrific because of the humid climate and the demands of physical labor. Those who aided runaways could be fined and jailed. In order to keep their activities as secret as possible, both runaways and Underground Railroad agents developed secret codes to hide their hopes for freedom and the details of their escape plans. Songs were an especially important means of communicating their intentions.

Slaves brought from Africa a time-honored tradition of communicating through music.[7] While slave owners quickly realized that drums were used for communication and outlawed them, slaves increasingly turned to songs and spirituals to share hidden messages. Songs, encoded in traditional lyrics, provided hope for freedom and practical advice for escape and went undetected by owners, who mistakenly believed that a singing slave was a happy one.[8]

You can use an audiotape of slave songs titled *Music and the Underground Railroad*.[9] Begin by playing the song "Go Down Moses," which sounds like the innocent recounting of a popular Biblical story. But when sung by slaves, the song held another meaning. After listening to the song, review the words line by line with students, encouraging them to discover the secret meaning. Students should pay special attention to the underlined words:

Go Down Moses

Song	Interpretation
When <u>Israel</u> was in <u>Egypt's land</u>,	Enslaved people / the South
Let my people go.	
Oppressed so hard they could not stand,	
Let my people go.	
Go down, <u>Moses</u>, way down in Egypt's land.	Harriet Tubman
Tell ole <u>pharaoh</u>,	Slave owner
Let my people go.	

"Go Down Moses" was a popular spiritual among slaves planning an escape. "Moses" referred to the biblical leader of the Israelite people as well as to Harriet Tubman, the so-called Moses of her people, or black slaves. "Pharaoh" was the slaveholder. "Egypt" was the South, where Tubman would travel to guide her people out of bondage and to freedom in the "Promised Land" of the North.[10]

"Follow the Drinking Gourd" was another popular song that gave practical advice for finding the way to freedom.

Follow the Drinking Gourd

Song	Interpretation
Follow the drinking gourd, follow the drinking gourd	
For the old man is a waiting for to carry us to freedom	
Follow the <u>drinking gourd</u>	The Big Dipper, a constellation of stars that resembles a drinking gourd
<u>When the sun goes down and the first quail calls</u>	Leave in the evening
Follow the drinking gourd	

For the old man is a-waitin' for to carry
    you to freedom
Follow the drinking gourd

<u>The river bank would make a mighty good road</u>	Walk in the river to confuse bloodhounds.
<u>Dead trees will show you the way</u>	Look for dead trees; moss grows on the *north* side.
<u>Left foot, peg foot traveling on</u>	Follow footprints of conductor Peg Leg Joe.
Follow the drinking gourd	
<u>The river ends between two hills</u>	Go to end of one river, walk between hills . . .
Follow the drinking gourd	
<u>There's another river on the other side</u>	. . . and follow the next river.
Follow the drinking gourd	

"Follow the Drinking Gourd" was a secret metaphor for the Big Dipper, a constellation of stars that resembles a gourd used to dip water from a bucket. The two stars on the outer side of the bowl point to the North Star, the only star whose position in the sky is fixed. By going in the direction of the North Star, runaways were heading north toward freedom (see Figure 5–2). Fugitives, not knowing whom to trust as they traveled across strange terrain, could follow the North Star over mountains, through valleys, and over other unfamiliar territory in their escape to freedom.

Other popular escape songs included "Wade in the Water," which was a warning to avoid slave hunters by preventing their bloodhounds from picking up a fugitive's scent, and "Let Us Break Bread Together," which directed slaves to meet before sunrise on the east side of the slave quarters to plan an escape.[11]

Drawing the Line: A Classroom Activity

On pages 108–10 are card illustrations of people whose lives were touched by the institution of slavery. Most of them lived or traveled on a section of the Eastern Line of the Underground Railroad between Wilmington, Delaware, and upstate New York. Each card contains a brief narrative telling the person's particular story. The decisions they made—principled or self-serving, courageous or cowardly—shaped the turbulent history of their time. Each of these individuals had to decide where to draw the line in acting on his or her beliefs about slavery. Should they choose peaceful or violent behavior?

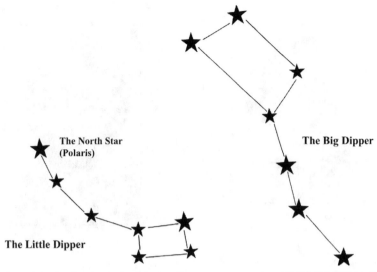

Figure 5–2. *The drinking gourd points north.*

Should they work within the boundaries of the civil law or defy it? How effective would their actions be in achieving their goals?

On the chalkboard create a sliding scale that looks like this:

Peaceful --- Violent

Legal --- Illegal

Effective --- Ineffective

Divide the class into small groups and assign each group one of the characters. Have each group read their narrative and judge their character's actions. Also have them consider the following question: If faced with similar circumstances, where would we draw the line? After allotting sufficient time for group discussion, have a spokesperson from each group read aloud the group's narrative and share their conclusions about their character's decision. Have another person from the group go to the chalkboard and draw a marking point on each scale to describe that decision and explain why the groups reached that conclusion.

As a follow-up activity or homework assignment, have the student pretend that they are living in the nineteenth century and have witnessed Underground Railroad activities. Allow them to choose one of the characters and write a short story or a play about that character and themselves. What advice would they give to the character? How would they help or prevent the character's Underground Railroad activities? What is the outcome?

Rachel Parker
House Maid

In 1851 a free black woman, Rachel Parker, sat in a Baltimore jail, awaiting sale into slavery. She had been kidnapped by Thomas McCreary from a farm in East Nottingham Township, Chester County, Pennsylvania. When a group of West Chester Quakers learned of her illegal capture, they raised $300 for Rachel's legal defense and succeeded in having her released.

Mose
Slave

Mose, a slave on a Mississippi plantation, attacked his overseer with a stake rather than accept a beating as punishment. Mose's master realized that he could not break the slave and instead auctioned him off.

Johnson Hayes Walker
Runaway Slave

For weeks a fugitive slave hid in the Kennett Square home of free black man, James Walker, while Dr. Isaac Johnson and nurse Esther Hayes visited regularly to tend to his injured foot. After the Civil War, a distinguished black man visited Kennett Square and introduced himself as Johnson Hayes Walker. As a free man the former slave had discarded his slave name and adopted the names of the three people in Kennett Square who helped him during his escape.

Mary
Runaway Slave

Mary, a 33 year-old slave of John Ennis of Georgetown, Delaware, came through West Chester, Pennsylvania, with her two daughters during her escape to Canada in 1854. Mary said she made the decision to escape because she feared that her daughters were to be sold further South.

Edward Gorsuch
Slaveholder

Violence erupted on September 11, 1851 when Baltimore slaveholder Edward Gorsuch and a small party of men including a deputy U. S. Marshall tried to recover his runaway slave from the home of William Parker, a free black stationmaster of Christiana, Lancaster County, Pennsylvania. Gorsuch was killed and his son was injured; Parker and those in his house escaped to Canada.

Henry "Box" Brown
Escaped Slave

Henry Brown, a slave in Richmond, Virginia, asked a friend to help him escape. Together the men decided to "mail" Henry to freedom in a wooden crate bound for Philadelphia. During the journey, the crate was lodged upside down, putting Brown on his head. He managed to survive, beginning his life as a free man when he was unpacked at the Pennsylvania Anti-Slavery Society.

Mary Ann Shadd
Esayist and Newspaper Publisher

Mary Ann Shadd of West Chester, Pennsylvania, was a mulatto, a person with both black and white ancestors. She chose to fight for the rights of black people by writing essays for the abolitionist newspaper The North Star. At age 28, Shadd moved to Canada where she founded an abolitionist newspaper, The Provincial Freeman.

Amos B. McFarlan
Kidnapper

Amos McFarlan of Downingtown, Pennsylvania, and his friend Solomon States promised a free black teenager a job as a coachman, but instead kidnapped him to be sold into slavery. When the boy proved that he was free, McFarlan was sentenced to six years in prison and fined $500.

Thomas Garrett
Merchant

Thomas Garrett, Quaker merchant of Wilmington, Delaware, worked with Harriet Tubman, William Still and local conductors to assist more than 2500 runaway slaves in their flight to freedom. Found guilty of harboring runaways in 1848, Garrett defiantly turned to the courtroom spectators and proclaimed, "If any of you know of any slave who needs assistance, send him to me."

Harriet Tubman
Underground Railroad Conductor

A single step changed Harriet Tubman's life forever. She had escaped from slavery in Dorchester County, Maryland, to the free state of Pennsylvania. Tubman recalled her first step over the Mason-Dixon Line, "There was such a glory over everything…and I felt like I was in heaven." Tubman returned to the South 19 times to lead others to freedom. Her courage in helping slaves escape earned her the affectionate title "Moses" among slaves and abolitionists.

Ann Preston
Physician

As a young girl, Ann Preston of West Grove, Chester County, Pennsylvania, found herself at home alone when a runaway slave came to her family's home with a slave catcher in close pursuit. Thinking quickly, Ann dressed the fugitive in her mother's clothes and the two of them rode in a wagon toward a Quaker Meeting. The slave catchers who saw them let them pass, thinking they were two Quakers on their way to worship.

William Still
Abolitionist

William Still, a free black man and Chairman of the Philadelphia Vigilance Committee of the Pennsylvania Anti-Slavery Society, arranged shelter and transportation for runaways who came through Philadelphia. Still recorded and later published the personal histories of the runaways.

Simulation Exercises

Middle school students love role playing, especially simulation games in which each student is assigned a specific role and must adhere to a particular set of interests for that role in a given situation. Teachers may want to return to the two escape stories given in Chapter 3—Henry Box Brown and Jane Johnson—and have the students write their own simulation, or play, based on those stories. Alternatively, here are four simulation exercises of varying degrees of complexity and preparation that are sure to arouse student curiosity about the Underground Railroad.

Simulation 1: The Escape of Rachel Harris

CHARACTERS

Mrs. Worthington/Stage Manager
Costume: a mob cap, or baggy
   cloth cap
Line: "Oh, come, Dear! You must
   be mistaken!" (cue card 5)

Rachel Harris, a former slave
Costume: apron
Line: "May I please step into the
   backyard?" (cue card 3)

A slave catcher
Costume: haversack, or a cloth
   handbag
Line: "I've found you!" (cue card 1)

A constable
Costume: a vest, hat
Line: "Wait! Stop!" (cue card 4)

Judge Thomas S. Bell
Costume: a quill pen, eyeglasses
Line: "Wait a minute—let's look at
   the facts." (cue card 2)

To Set the Stage
Teacher/narrator sits on a chair stage right; chair for Mrs. Worthington is at stage left, with a man's hat and vest hidden behind the chair.

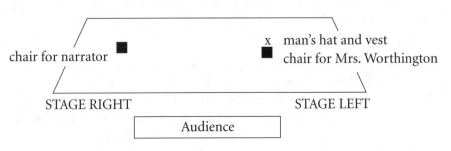

Introduction

NARRATOR (TEACHER): This is a true story about an African American woman named Rachel Harris who lived before the Civil War. We know Rachel's story because in 1839 a newspaperman in Chester County, Pennsylvania wrote about her and, after the Civil War, historians published her story in books.[12] But none of these accounts includes all the details. We don't know, for example, exactly what Rachel said at every moment, but we can imagine that her adventure went much like the story that I'm about to tell. I'm going to need everyone's help to tell this story. Some of you will need to play parts in the story. *(Select volunteers for each part and assign costumes and cue cards; place actors on stage as illustrated below.)*

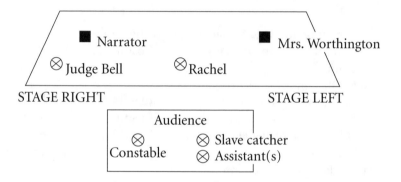

Some of you have lines to say, written down on cue cards. I'll let you know when to say your lines. The rest of you have lines to say as well. Once while I'm telling the story, I'm going to ask, "Where, oh, where did Rachel Harris go?" Then I want you all to say, "She went that way!" and point to the back of the room. Let's practice. Where, oh, where did Rachel Harris go?

STUDENTS: She went that way! *(pointing behind them to the back of the room)*

NARRATOR: Good! Now, that part isn't going to come until near the end of the story, so don't forget!

The Story

NARRATOR: And now for our story. Rachel was a tall, strong woman who loved to sing and tell stories. She was a slave when she was young and lived in Maryland. Her master there was cruel and he forced her to work very hard for no pay. But then one day Rachel ran away to the North, where slavery was against the law. Eventually she came to live in West Chester, Pennsylvania, where she married a man named Isaac Harris.

In West Chester, Rachel worked as a laundress, washing clothes for other families. Her hard work earned the respect of many people in the town, and for about five years, Rachel lived in West Chester free from slavery. But her old slave master was angry that Rachel had run away, and he announced that he would give a large reward to anyone who could tell him where to find Rachel. After about five years, somebody decided to tell on Rachel and take the reward. A man came to West Chester to capture Rachel Harris and take her back into slavery. *(Slave catcher stands up.)* He found a constable to help him. *(Constable stands up.)* The men went to Rachel Harris' house, and before Rachel could run away, they arrested her. *(Slave catcher and Constable stand by Rachel.)* The slave catcher said:

SLAVE CATCHER: I've found you!

NARRATOR: They took her to the house of a judge named Thomas Bell and asked the judge for justice. *(Slave catcher and Constable guide Rachel to stand in front of Judge Bell, who is standing by Narrator.)* The slave catcher said that Rachel should be returned to her owner and become a slave again.

Judge Bell knew that the law said that this man was right, but Judge Bell did not want to let them take Rachel away from West Chester. He believed that slavery was wrong. He tried to stall for time. Judge Bell said:

JUDGE BELL: Wait a minute—let's look at the facts.

NARRATOR: Rachel was worried that she would be brought back into slavery if she didn't do something quick. Rachel said:

RACHEL: May I please step into the backyard?

TEACHER/NARRATOR: There was no toilet in Judge Bell's house. The men assumed that Rachel needed to use the outhouse, or "necessary," in the backyard. So the constable followed her out behind the house. *(Rachel and Constable walk around to stand on the other side of Narrator.)* Rachel looked around. The backyard was surrounded by a tall fence—much taller than Rachel or the constable. The constable waited for Rachel. *(Narrator whispers in Rachel's ear, instructing Rachel to run away into the audience—now!)* And then Rachel made a big jump, climbed over the fence, and ran away before the constable even knew what was going on! The constable said:

CONSTABLE: Wait! Stop!

NARRATOR: But the constable could not catch Rachel. He couldn't jump over that fence. He got out to the street and then started running after her, but he was too far behind.

Rachel Harris ran away through the streets of West Chester. She ran through a hat-making shop, where she managed to jump over a big vat of boiling liquid. She came to a house where the Worthingtons lived. *(Rachel stands by Mrs. Worthington.)* Rachel had done laundry for Mrs. Worthington, and Rachel begged to hide in the house. At first Mrs. Worthington did not believe that a slave catcher was chasing Rachel. Mrs. Worthington said:

MRS. WORTHINGTON: Oh, come, Dear! You must be mistaken!

NARRATOR: But then Mrs. Worthington saw how scared Rachel was. Mrs. Worthington agreed to hide Rachel in a cubbyhole in the attic. *(Mrs. Worthington has Rachel hide behind her.)*

The constable could not find Rachel. He gave up and went back to get the slave catcher to help. The constable, the slave catcher, and his assistants looked all over West Chester. They found an old man on the street and asked him if he had seen a woman running away. That old man had seen Rachel running toward the Worthington's house, but he didn't want to tell that to the slave catchers.

The slave catchers asked, "Where, oh, where did Rachel Harris go?"

STUDENTS: She went that way! *(pointing to the back of the room) (At this time Rachel changes into the men's clothes while remaining hidden behind Mrs. Worthington's chair.)*

NARRATOR: —said the old man. So the slave catchers followed the man's directions and went looking in the wrong direction, and they couldn't find her anywhere. *(Slave catchers sit down.)*

But Rachel knew that she couldn't hide in Mrs. Worthington's attic forever. So, she made plans for her and her husband to escape to Canada, where the slave catchers couldn't get them. First she and Isaac would have to leave West Chester without being noticed; the slave catcher was looking for her all over town. She got help from several people in West Chester who were part of the Underground Railroad.

One evening, Rachel dressed up as a man so that the slave catcher wouldn't recognize her, and she and her husband were able to walk through town to meet a carriage that brought them safely out of West Chester. *(Rachel stands up and walks to the back of the room.)* They stayed in a friend's house there for a while, and then they traveled to Canada, where Rachel Harris was finally able to be truly free.

THE END

Questions for Discussion

1. Do you think that Judge Bell wanted Rachel to escape? If so, wasn't he breaking the very same Fugitive Slave Law he was sworn to uphold as a judge?

2. What kinds of clues does the Rachel Harris escape give us about the operation of the Underground Railroad?

3. Rewrite the ending of the story: what happens to Rachel if the slave catcher takes her back into slavery?

Simulation 2: The Story of Ruth: A Girl Who Helped on the Underground Railroad

Instructions for Teacher

This play is meant to be performed in the classroom with minimal or no rehearsal. The adult leader serves as narrator and provides cues and stage directions to the young actors as the play progresses. Each actor has only one line, and the actors carry cue cards that indicate what their lines are. The diagram that follows indicates where the actors should stand at the start of the play.

CHARACTERS

- An adult **narrator**

- **Ruth**—a young Quaker woman whose father is an abolitionist (cue card 4: "There. Now thee will pass for Mother.") **costume**: mob cap, scoop bonnet

- **Benny**—Ruth's brother (cue card 1: "Do not fear, Ruth. I will try to find one of our good neighbors to help.") **costume**: vest

- **Mr. Jackson**—a neighbor and fellow abolitionist (cue card 2: "Hello Ruth! I came to warn you; the slave woman's master is coming!) **costume**: Quaker hat

- A **voice** heard by Ruth (cue card 3: "Thy people meet today.")

- An **escaped black slave woman** (cue card 5: "I pray this disguise will not fail.") **costume**: shawl, bonnet with veil to be put on during play

- The woman's **slave owner** (cue card 6: "Halt! We're looking for a runaway slave. We need to search through your wagon.") **costume**: planter's hat

- A **slave catcher** (cue card 7: "Well, well, this little girl and her mother here must be going to Quaker meeting. Looks as if they are going to get there late today.") **costume**: haversack

---

⊗ Escaped slave	※ two chairs,
⊗ Narrator (seated)	※ representing
	wagon seats
⊗ A voice Ruth ⊗ ⊗ Benny	
STAGE	

AUDIENCE	
⊗ Jackson	⊗ Slave catchers
	⊗ Slave owner

Introduction

This is a story about a young woman named Ruth who helped a black slave woman to escape from her slave owner on the Underground Railroad. The Underground Railroad was not under the ground, and it was not a train at all; it was a secret network of safe places where escaped slaves could hide as they traveled north to freedom.

This story comes from a poem that a female doctor named Ann Preston wrote more than one hundred years ago. Ann Preston did not make up this story—it happened to her when she was young; Ann just decided to change the name of the heroine to Ruth. [13]

> NARRATOR: It was a beautiful spring day in West Grove, Pennsylvania, in 1836. Robins were flying through the air, and the maple trees were just beginning to show leaves. It was Sunday. Usually Ruth attended Quaker meeting on Sunday, but today she was at home, caring for the family farm. Her father and mother had left yesterday to go to a big quarterly meeting of the Quakers, so she and her brother Benny would have to handle things on their own.
>
> Today Ruth and Benny had something big to handle; there was a runaway slave woman hiding in their attic. Ruth's parents worked on the Underground Railroad, and this slave woman

needed a safe place to hide. Ruth knew that if the slave catchers found this woman she would be forced back into cruel slavery. Ruth also knew that her whole family could get in trouble if anyone found out that they were helping a runaway slave.

Ruth was worried, and she told her brother Benny that she wished that her mother and father were home. Benny said:

BENNY: Do not fear, Ruth. I will try to find one of our good neighbors to help.

NARRATOR: Benny walked off to look for help. *(Benny can sit down in the audience now.)* Ruth watched and worried. As she waited, a man came galloping up on a horse. It was her neighbor, Mr. Jackson. *(Mr. Jackson should get up now and rush to stand by Ruth.)* He was riding fast, but he stopped as soon as he reached Ruth. He spoke in a hurried voice. Mr. Jackson said:

MR. JACKSON: Hello, Ruth! I came to warn you; the slave woman's master is coming!

NARRATOR: Mr. Jackson rode off to warn the neighbors. *(Mr. Jackson can sit down in the audience now.)* Ruth was frightened to stay alone at the house. She was worried about what the slave catchers might do if they came and found the slave woman hiding here. Ruth did not know what to do, but then she got a sudden inspiration. She heard a low voice say something. The voice said:

VOICE: Thy people meet today.

NARRATOR: "That's right"! Ruth remembered. "Today is Sunday. Most of the Friends are at Quaker meeting today!" Ruth came up with a plan to help the slave woman escape. She climbed up the stairs, and the escaped slave woman came out of hiding. The woman looked very frightened. *(Escaped slave woman can stand next to Ruth now.)* Ruth changed her own mob cap for a bonnet. *(Ruth changes her own mob cap for a bonnet.)* Then she took one of her mother's gowns, a shawl, and a bonnet with a thick green veil and gave them to the slave woman. The slave woman put on the bonnet and veil so that her face was completely covered. *(Escaped slave woman puts on costume.)* Ruth was pleased. Ruth said:

RUTH: There. Now thee will pass for Mother.

NARRATOR: With the slave woman disguised as Ruth's mother, Ruth and the woman walked carefully out of the house. Ruth hitched the horse to the wagon, and she started driving herself and the slave woman away on the wagon, as if she were driving to Quaker meeting with her mother. *(Ruth and escaped slave woman sit in "wagon."*) The woman was even more frightened now. In a quiet voice, the slave woman said:

ESCAPED SLAVE WOMAN: I pray this disguise will not fail.

NARRATOR: Ruth knew that both she and the woman were in great danger now. She drove farther from home, and just then, several men came riding toward them at great speed. *(Slave owner and Slave catcher can stand up from the audience now and hurry to stand by Ruth and escaped slave woman.)* Ruth grew pale. The slave woman trembled. It was her slave owner and a slave catcher. The slave owner said:

SLAVE OWNER: Halt! We're looking for a runaway slave. We need to search through your wagon.

NARRATOR: The men climbed all over the wagon, looking for any hidden passengers. But they barely looked at Ruth or the woman in disguise. After a while, they gave up. One of the slave catchers said:

SLAVE CATCHER: Well, well, this little girl and her mother here must be going to Quaker meeting. Looks as if they are going to get there late today.

NARRATOR: With that, the slave catchers and the slave owner went riding hurriedly off, still looking for the escaped slave woman. *(Slave catcher and Slave owner can sit back down in the audience now.)* Ruth drove on to Mr. Jackson's house in safety and left the slave woman there to be taken care of by the Jackson family. *(Escaped slave woman goes to sit with Mr. Jackson.)* Then Ruth started driving home.

And great was her rejoicing
As she took her homeward way
That she had foiled the hunters
And snatched from them, their prey.

The End

Questions for Discussion

1. What kinds of clues does the story give us about the operation of the Underground Railroad?

2. Why did the slave catchers fall for Ruth's ploy? Did they trust that Quakers wouldn't help runaways? Why didn't they lift the bonnet of the disguised runaway slave?

3. Rewrite the ending of the story: what happens to Ruth if she is caught aiding a runaway slave?

These skits can be used by both teachers and students as models to create their own plays. Information can be taken from the historical survey provided in Chapter 1 and used for the general context of the play, while the character sketches provided in the Drawing the Line activity can give students ideas for the specific roles they might want to assume in their own plays.

Simulation 3: Shopping Your Conscience

This activity illustrates the important economic impact of slave-produced goods in the years before the Civil War. By 1840 the value of cotton exports exceeded all other exports by 52 percent. Two decades later, in 1860, the value of slaves exceeded the value of all railroads, banks, and factories combined in the United States. Slave labor produced many everyday items found in the general stores of the North. While many Northern consumers fooled themselves into believing that purchasing slave produce did not mean they were supporting the peculiar institution, other consumers made sure that their actions were consistent with their abolitionist beliefs by refusing to buy any products made by slave labor. Here's a plan to teach this lesson.

Step 1:

Create a class general store by asking students to bring in the following items from home, with the exception of tobacco, which should be simulated. Once all items are collected, you should identify each one with one of the following labels:

> tobacco from Virginia
>
> rice from South Carolina
>
> sugar from Cuba
>
> cotton fabric, grown in Mississippi
>
> coffee from Brazil
>
> New Jersey apples
>
> Wisconsin butter
>
> New York State cheese
>
> wool fabric from New Hampshire sheep
>
> linen made from Pennsylvania flax
>
> honey, made in Vermont
>
> Pennsylvania eggs

Step 2:

Assign twelve students to do research on how a specific product was made during the first part of the nineteenth century. These students will later play the role of worker/producer and briefly explain to the class their findings. For example, the Pennsylvania farm girl would describe how she and her family do all the work on their farm, and that one of her daily chores is to collect the eggs from the chicken coop and put them in small cartons for her father to sell at the local farmer's market. She might also explain how much her family earns from that produce and how they spend the money. Another student, playing the role of a Mississippi field slave, would describe the grueling process of working twelve- to fourteen-hour days planting and harvesting cotton in temperatures that routinely rise above ninety-five degrees. He would also explain that he isn't paid for his labor and that his master considers his responsibility to the slave as providing the slave with food, clothing, and shelter.

Step 3:

Set up a general store for the following day's class, complete with two or three shopping baskets and the following six shopping lists.

Shopping List 1	*Shopping List 2*	*Shopping List 3*
sugar	wool fabric	tobacco
coffee	butter	sugar
apples	cheese	cotton fabric
cheese	rice	butter

Shopping List 4	*Shopping List 5*	*Shopping List 6*
honey	tobacco	apples
coffee	rice	butter
apples	sugar	cheese
eggs	cotton fabric	wool fabric

Step 4:

On the day of the lesson, give each shopping list to a student who has not been assigned a worker/producer role and have the shoppers fill their market baskets at the general store. After each basket is filled, ask the student to determine which items were produced by free labor and which were slave-made and sort them into slave-labor and free-labor piles. Ask those who have slave-made items if they still want to purchase them and why or why not.

Step 5:

Ask the worker/producer of each item to make his or her presentation. Return to those students who initially said they would still purchase the slave-made goods. Have they changed their minds after hearing these presentations? If so, ask them what alternative product—made by free labor—they might use a replacement.

Step 6:

Conduct a class discussion based on the following questions.

1. If you buy objects made by slaves, are you in any way supporting slavery?

2. Refusing to buy slave-made products was a kind of *boycott,* designed to make slave ownership unprofitable. What makes an effective boycott?

3. If you chose to boycott slave-made products to show your opposition to slavery, which slave-made products would be difficult for you to give up?

4. Could you find any free-labor substitutes for slave-labor products?

5. Can you think of any products that are boycotted today? Why? Consider some of the labor practices in South America, where children are employed to manufacture clothing and/or footwear for extremely low wages. Migrant farm workers in the United States are also paid extremely low wages to plant and harvest such produce as lettuce and grapes.

Living History

Living history has, over the last decade, become one of the most popular educational and entertaining movements in our country. The National Park Service, Civil War reenactors, and individual educator-historians use living history to challenge their audiences to think and feel in ways that make the past come alive. Unlike traditional academic history, the practitioners of living history believe that the past can be inspirational as well as factual and that engaging the empathy of others is every bit as important as helping them understand history. This does not mean that accuracy is compromised for entertainment. Instead the challenge for a reenactor is to understand and present the people and events of the past as honestly and accurately as possible. This involves integrating into the performance people's own words and experiences, taken from letters, diaries, journals, or speeches. In this way, the reenactor can become part of another generation for the audience while recognizing that to do so completely is impossible. This is a matter of respecting the historical integrity of the subject itself.

I have used living history as a means of engaging middle school students, both as a teacher and as a museum educator. One of the most inspirational performances is Levi Coffin, an Ohio Quaker who was known as the president of the Underground Railroad.

Most of the script was paraphrased from Coffin's *Reminiscences,* published in 1876. I have reprinted the script of this performance in its entirety in the hope of encouraging readers to rehearse and perform it for their students. You will need the following props and costumes:

1 broad-brimmed hat, dark suit of clothing, and white, button-down shirt *(to be worn by Levi Coffin)*

2 additional large, white-button-down shirts for student performers *(laborers' shirts for two male student performers)*

1 pair of makeshift slave shackles—two cardboard wrist cuffs joined with a metal chain

1 garden rake *(farm tool)*

1 woman's shawl *(for female student playing slave mistress)*

1 woman's bonnet that can be scooped down over the face of a female student performer *(for slave mistress)*

Levi Coffin: President of the Underground Railroad

(Speak in a firm but soft voice.) Friends, I have been moved by the Lord to remark on the circumstances of my life. My name is Levi Coffin and I was born in 1798 to Levi and Prudence Coffin, Quakers of New Garden, North Carolina. *(Recall with a feeling of nostalgia)* I was raised according to the testimonies of Friends. From an early age I wore the plain dress, or black and white clothing and broad-brimmed hat, that are the peculiar badges of the Quaker religion. But it was in my heart and in my actions that I really let my life speak. Among those testimonies I held most dear was the equality of all human beings, regardless of their race, creed, or gender. I had difficulty understanding how a black slave could be treated as the property of his white owner.

(More slowly, subdued) When I was seven years old, my father and I were chopping wood on our farm when a group of slaves came by on the road. They were all chained together so none could escape. My father told me that they were being taken to the auction block to be sold and probably would never see their wives or children again. Any time any one of 'em talked the slave driver would beat 'em with a leather whip. I just couldn't imagine what it would be like to be separated from my parents. I guess I knew in my heart at that point that I was going to be an abolitionist and help these poor people gain their freedom.

(Take out makeshift shackles—wrist cuffs made of cardboard joined together by chains.) Does anybody know what these are? *(Listen to student responses; pick up on the "handcuff" response.)* Yes, they're like handcuffs, but they are called shackles, and there is a major difference. What kind of people wear handcuffs? *(Listen for a "criminal" response.)* Yes, criminals, people who

commit a crime against society. Who wore shackles? *(Listen for "slaves" response.)* I ask you, what crime has the slave committed? *(Students will probably say none.)* What if he runs away? What crime has he committed then? *(Listen to student responses. See if anyone can make the connection between a slave's status as property and stealing—a slave is stealing his master's property if he runs away. If no one does, explain it.)* According to the United States Constitution, during the first half of the nineteenth century, a slave was the property of his white master. If he ran away, then he was stealing his master's property. Not only that, but if you, as a United States citizen, refused to assist in the slave's recapture, you could be fined up to one thousand dollars and jailed for up to six months time. Those were the rules according to the Fugitive Slave Law of 1793. *(Hold up makeshift shackles.)* These, my young friends, are nothing more than a painful symbol of man's inhumanity to his fellow man and, when I was fifteen years old, I promised the Lord that I would do everything in my power to put an end to their use.

In 1819 the United States Congress passed a law called the Missouri Compromise, which stated that if you lived north of the Ohio River, you couldn't own any more slaves. This law led to the creation of free states in the North and slave states in the South. The law went into effect the following year and six years later, in 1826, my wife, Catharine, and I moved to Newport, Indiana. There, I opened a grocery store and started a linseed oil mill that produced colorful paints. We also opened our home as a station on the Underground Railroad.

Now who can tell us what the Underground Railroad was? *(Listen to student responses.)* Actually, the name itself gives you a pretty good definition. The word *underground* suggests something that is invisible, or something that is secret, and *railroad* is a method of transportation. So the Underground Railroad was a secret or invisible method of transportation for slaves running away from the South to freedom in the North. Like the railroads of today, the Underground Railroad also had *stations*. These were the homes of abolitionists like myself who gave food and shelter to the runaways. Like the railroads, we also had *conductors* who would transport runaways between stations, usually under the cover of darkness and always traveling north. But sometimes, if a slave catcher was in close pursuit of a runaway, we had to move them in broad daylight. Now I want to show you how this was done, but I'm going to need some volunteers.

(Choose a boy from the audience and give him an oversized, button-down shirt and a rake or other farm tool.) Often, I would disguise a runaway as a laborer, having him carry a rake on his shoulder so he wouldn't look suspicious. Everyone knows that slave owners sometimes hired out their slaves to make extra money for themselves. *(Looking to the male student volunteer)*

Now, you are going to play the runaway, disguised as a hired-out laborer. I will play the slave catcher and the audience will be the jury. They will decide how convincing your explanation is when I stop you. Your responsibility is to talk yourself out of being taken back into slavery. Ready?

(Listen to student's explanation. Consider the following:

- *Does he offer you money? Bribes were common among runaways. The money was given by an Underground Railroad agent. If the amount was sufficient, a slave catcher would often accept it.*
- *Does he have papers from his master—forged or real—that would explain his being hired out? If so, let him go.*
- *Other convincing stories are that he is lost or that he is returning to his master's plantation.)*

(Ask students in audience how convincing the performance was. If they don't think it was convincing, have them offer a possible story.)

(Now select two other male students and a female. Dress the boys as laborers and the female as a Southern plantation mistress.)

(To student performers) You two boys are accompanying your mistress to the North. In fact, all three of you are runaway slaves. Now, if the slave mistress, who is really a black runaway slave, is to be convincing, what can I not see? *(Students should answer face and any part of her skin.)* So, I am going to disguise her with a shawl and a scoop bonnet that I will pull down over her face.

(To student audience) What can I not hear? *(Listen for students to say voice.)* Right, her voice would give her away. Her two servants will have to do her talking for her. *(To student performers)* Now you three go over in the corner and concoct a story. *(Give them two or three minutes to arrive at a strategy.)*

(To student audience) Just to put our skit in a proper historical perspective, I should mention that during the early years of the Underground Railroad, most of the runaways were single young men between the ages of eighteen and thirty-five. They had the physical endurance to make a long journey and they did not have the responsibility of raising a family. Women, on the other hand, had the primary responsibility for caring for children in the slave community, whether they were married or not. So it was not too common for women to run away. But after 1850, with the passage of a strong Fugitive Slave Law and increased kidnappings, it was more common for women and even entire families to run away. This next skit illustrates an escape that would have taken place after 1850.

(To student performers) Are you ready? Remember, you are three runaway slaves, disguised as a Southern plantation mistress and her two slaves. I will play the slave catcher.

(Dialogue with the students. See how they get themselves out of the situation. Common resolutions are that the mistress has a contagious disease and is being taken to a doctor in the North. Bribery is another option. Thank the students and let them return to their seats.)

Sometimes I would mount a team of horses to a false-bottomed wagon and carry the runaways myself to the next station. As long as they were hidden under the false floorboards, and that false floor was piled high with hay or other produce, the runaways were safe from being discovered. The ultimate destination was Canada.

I've been told that I have helped about one hundred slaves escape from bondage each year for twenty years. Some folks estimate that I have helped as many as four thousand runaways and, being much impressed, gave me the name President of the Underground Railroad. Regardless of how many slaves I assisted in gaining their freedom, I couldn't have done much at all if not for the ingenuity and determination of the runaways themselves. Let me close with the story of Eliza Harris, one of the most determined runaways I'd ever known.

In 1841 Catharine and I moved to Cincinnati to start a free-labor grocery store, that is, a store that sold items that were made by free instead of slave labor. Because Cincinnati was located on the Ohio River, which divided the free states of the North and the slaves states of the South, there was an active Underground Railroad network there, too. It was during my years in Cincinnati that I met Eliza Harris.

Eliza was a slave from Kentucky who lived quite close to the Ohio River. Her master fell into financial debt and planned to sell Eliza and her two-year-old son. When she found out about his intentions she grabbed the baby boy and ran for the river, with slave catchers in pursuit. It was the winter and parts of the Ohio had frozen over, but at other points there were chunks of floating ice.

(With growing emotion, excitement) It was dangerous to cross, but Eliza knew she must get to the other side with her baby or die trying. Holding her baby tight in one arm she jumped out onto a piece of ice, no bigger than a tabletop, and continued to jump from one piece of ice to the next. Somehow, she made it across. When she came to me she was totally exhausted and nearly frozen. We nursed her back to health and moved her on to safety in Canada.

(More composed) I tell you her story because I think it gives you an idea of just how desperate some people were to enjoy the very same freedom we all seem to take for granted today.

In closing, let me just say that some people still ask me why I helped runaway slaves when it was against the law. I did it for a reason that is just as relevant today as it was during my lifetime *(Speak very slowly and with emphasis)* I did it because as long as there is a single individual in this country who is deprived of his or her God-given freedoms, then none of us—none of you—is ever truly free.

Many of the stories in this play can be adapted by teachers interested in performing other abolitionist figures such as Harriet Tubman, Lucretia Mott, William Still, and Thomas Garrett. Research on these figures can be completed using some of the biographies and other sources listed in the bibliography. Following are some suggestions for writing and performing a play.

Writing a Living History Play

1. Establish a cause-and-effect story. The play has to hold student interest and explain why the subject took a certain course of action. This allows you, the actor or actress, to develop the Underground Railroad agent's story as you understand it.

2. Integrate anecdotes. Remember that stories, whether actual, embellished, or invented, always capture student interest.

3. Find a role model at the video store. Use movies and a particular actor to give you a better idea of how you might want to portray an Underground Railroad agent. This may include the accent you use, idiosyncratic behaviors, or a decision-making process. For example, Ed Asner in *Whispers of Angels* provides a convincing portrayal of Thomas Garrett. See the videography on pages 135–36 to discover other characters you might want to play.

Performing the Play

1. Gauge the play to run no more than twenty minutes so you can have class time to discuss it. You will most likely go over the time limit.

2. Exploit one or two of the characteristics or idiosyncrasies of the Underground Railroad agent you are portraying throughout the play. Still and Garrett, for example, tended to hold the lapels of their suit coat whenever they addressed an audience. Mott and Tubman tended to look directly into the face of the person with whom they were talking. Relying on these kinds of idiosyncrasies can make your portrayal more convincing.

3. Don't get caught up in the script. Yes, you will have to commit to memory some of the script. But allow your own interpretation of the character and your understanding of his or her emotions to carry the play.

4. Rehearse, rehearse, rehearse—and do it in front of a mirror before you try it in front of a live audience.

Summary

Class activities, decoding slave songs, simulations, and living history all have the potential to show students the practical and enjoyable application of history to their own lives. To be sure, the particular stories of the Underground Railroad differed from region to region, but creative teachers can adapt these activities to meet their own interests and needs. The key to a successful experience is student engagement and cultivating the critical thinking and empathy-building skills students will need to become constructive members of our multicultural society.

At the same time these exercises provide a nice complement to the more academically challenging ones provided in the earlier sections of the book. Together, they provide a dynamic curriculum that will engage students and pique their curiosity for further study on this important chapter of American history.

Endnotes

1. See Mauritz Johnson, ed., *Toward Adolescence: The Middle School Years.* (Chicago: University of Chicago, 1980).

2. See Erik Erikson, *Youth, Identity and Crisis.* (New York: Norton, 1968); Jerome Kagan and Robert Coles, eds., *Twelve to Sixteen: Early Adolescence* (New York: Norton, 1972); and William Alexander and Paul George, *The Exemplary Middle School* (New York: Holt, Rinehart and Winston, 1981).

3. Frederick Douglass, *Narrative of the Life of Frederick Douglass, An American Slave* (1845) (New York: Dover, 1995 reprint): 52.

4. Harriet Tubman quoted in Sarah Bradford, *Harriet Tubman: The Moses of Her People* (1886) (Bedford, MA: Applewood, 1993 reprint), 31–32.

5. Henry Ferry quoted in Charles L. Perdue, et al., eds., *Weevils in the Wheat: Interviews with Virginia Ex-Slaves* (Charlotte: University Press of Virginia, 1976), 91.

6. John A. Hunter quoted in Benjamin Drew, *Narratives of Fugitive Slaves* (1856) (Toronto: Prospero, 2000 reprint), 114.

7. Brenda E. Stevenson, "Slavery in America," in *Underground Railroad* (Washington, DC: National Park Service, 1998), 40–41.

8. John W. Blassingame, *The Slave Community: Plantation Life in the Antebellum South* (New York: Oxford University Press, 1972), 66–74; and Dena J. Epstein, "Slave Music in the United States Before 1860: A Survey of Sources," *Music Library Association Notes* XX (Spring 1963): 195–212.

9. *Music and the Underground Railroad* is available through Appleseed Recordings, P.O. Box 2593, West Chester, Pennsylvania 19380. Phone: (610) 701-5755. Fax: (610) 701-9599. Email: *FOLKRADICL@aol.com.*

10. Charles L. Blockson, "Escape from Slavery: The Underground Railroad," *National Geographic* (July 1984): 39; Charles L. Blockson, *African Americans in Pennsylvania: A History and Guide* (Baltimore: Black Classic, 1994), 12–13; Kim Harris and Reggie Harris, *Music and the Underground Railroad* (Philadelphia: Ascension, 1984); and Jacqueline L. Tobin and Raymond G. Dobard, "Steal Away," in *Hidden in Plain View*, 129–152.

11. Harris and Harris, *Music and the Underground Railroad*.

12. See "The Escape of Rachel Harris as Told by Her Master in West Chester, 1839," *Daily Local News* (West Chester, PA): September 27, 1883; see also Graceanna Lewis, "Cunningham's Rache" quoted in William Still, *The Underground Railroad*, (1872) (Chicago: Johnson, 1970 reprint), 781–83.

13. See Ann Preston, M.D., "Ruth—A Ballad of 1836," Chester County Historical Society Collections, West Chester, PA.

Annotated Bibliography

This annotated bibliography offers background reading for teachers and source material to complete the various activities provided in this book. Although some of these resources may go out of print, they can often be found at your local public library. Please note that this is *not* an exhaustive bibliography of the Underground Railroad, but one that I believe will be useful in making the subject engaging for middle school students.

Readings for Teachers

Bacon, Margaret H. 1980. *Valiant Friend: The Life of Lucretia Mott*. New York: Walker and Co.

Biography of Lucretia Mott (1792–1880), a feisty, brilliant, quick-witted Philadelphia Quaker and antebellum reformer. Chronicles her activities in abolitionism, health care, and women's rights.

Blockson, Charles L. 1987. *The Underground Railroad*. New York: Berkley.

A collection of first-person narratives, grouped along state lines, that describe the experiences of runaway slaves who used the Underground Railroad.

Blockson, Charles L. 1994. *Hippocrene Guide to the Underground Railroad*. New York: Hippocrene.

A travel guide and reference source to more than two hundred houses, buildings, and markers throughout the United States that are related to the Underground Railroad. Many of the sites are maintained by museums and historical societies. Includes a special Harriet Tubman Trail that identifies the route she took to free herself, her family, and other slaves.

Bradford, Sarah H. (1869) 1961. *Harriet Tubman: The Moses of Her People.* Reprint. Secaucus, NY: Citadel.

An early biography of Harriet Tubman (1821?–1913) based largely on recollections given by Tubman to the author. Contains an appendix of letters from prominent abolitionists Gerritt Smith, Wendell Phillips, and Frederick Douglass.

Cary, Lorene. 1995. *The Price of a Child.* New York: Vintage.

A fictionalized account of a young woman, traveling with her slave owner and two of her three children, who takes the bold step of declaring her freedom and beginning a new life as a free woman. Her only regret is that her youngest child is with her owner's wife in Virginia and may be sold off as a result of her actions. Philadelphia in 1855 is the main setting for the novel, which is based on the true story of William Still's daring rescue of Jane Johnson.

Coffin, Levi. 1876. *Reminiscences.* Cincinnati: Western Tract Society.

Levi Coffin (1798–1877) was considered the president of the Underground Railroad for having assisted in the escape of more than two thousand fugitive slaves. His book of reminiscences, moving at times and humorous at others, details his activities on the clandestine route to freedom. A print copy can be obtained from the Levi Coffin House website, *www.waynet.org/nonprofit/coffin.htm.*

Franklin, John Hope, and Loren Schweninger. 1999. *Runaway Slaves: Rebels on the Plantation.* New York: Oxford University Press.

Based on planters' records, petitions to county courts and state legislatures, and runaway slave advertisements, this precedent-setting study discusses the flight of slaves as a form of dissent. The reactions of white slaveholders and their attempts to prevent runaways are also discussed.

Gara, Larry. 1961. *The Liberty Line: The Legend of the Underground Railroad.* Lexington: University of Kentucky Press.

A major study of the Underground Railroad that debunks many of its myths and legends.

Gara makes important distinctions between the motives and goals of black and white abolitionists, showing that there was no unified position on how to achieve emancipation, even among the radicals who were its strongest advocates.

Horton, James O., and Lois E. Horton. 1997. *In Hope of Liberty: Culture, Community and Protest Among Northern Free Blacks, 1700–1860*. New York: Oxford University Press.

The standard work on the northern free black experience from 1700 to the Civil War. Contains important information on the relationship of the free black community to the antislavery movement, the Underground Railroad, and their enslaved brethren.

Mayer, Henry. 1998. *All On Fire: William Lloyd Garrison and the Abolition of Slavery*. New York: St. Martin's.

An excellent biography on America's foremost agitator and crusading journalist, William Lloyd Garrison (1805–1879). Mayer explains how Garrison inspired two generations of activists—female and male, black and white—to challenge the dominant assumptions of white supremacy in antebellum America and force change upon a reluctant majority.

McGowan, James A. 2004. *Station Master on the Underground Railroad: The Life and Letters of Thomas Garrett*. Jefferson, NC: McFarland.

A biography of Quaker abolitionist Thomas Garrett (1789–1871), who assisted more than twenty-seven hundred slaves in their escape to freedom. Garrett's personality and relationship with the free black community are chronicled in the broader context of the Underground Railroad's Eastern Line.

National Park Service. 1998. *Underground Railroad: Official National Park Handbook*. Washington, DC: U.S. Printing Office.

Three essays that provide a fine introduction to the topics of American slavery, the myth of the Underground Railroad, and the operation of the clandestine route to freedom.

Siebert, Wilbur H. (1898) 1967. *The Underground Railroad: From Slavery to Freedom*. Reprint. New York: Arno and The New York Times.

A pioneering study of the Underground Railroad that sheds light on its overall operation.

Still, William. (1872) 1970. *The Underground Railroad*. Reprint. Chicago: Johnson.

The classic study of the Underground Railroad's Eastern Line. Draws on William Still's (1821–1902) interviews of fugitives he aided in Philadelphia and correspondence from other agents.

Books for Middle Schoolers

Asante, Molefi Kete. 2002. *African American History: A Journey of Liberation.* Saddlebrook, NJ: Peoples.

A comprehensive textbook written by a leading revisionist. Unit 7, titled "Contesting Enslavement, 1763–1890," addresses the Underground Railroad. Asante encourages students to think about multiple perspectives on the clandestine route to freedom and its effectiveness by offering different accounts of the abolitionist movement. Important connections are also made between African American and global history. Best for Grades 4–8.

Ayres, Katherine. 2000. *North by Night: A Story of the Underground Railroad.* Reed Business Information.

An amazing story of personal growth about a girl who works with her family, who are stationmasters. She learns what it means to give up all you know for another person. Grades 5–8.

Banta, Melissa. 1993. *Frederick Douglass: Voice of Liberty.* Chelsea House.

Biography of a man who, after escaping slavery, became an orator, writer, and leader in the antislavery movement in the nineteenth century. Good black-and-white artwork and photographs. Includes further reading list, chronology, glossary, and index. Grades 4–8.

Bentley, Judith. 1997. "*Dear Friend*": *Thomas Garrett and William Still, Collaborators on the Underground Railroad.* New York: Cobblehill/ Dutton.

The story of a white Quaker, Thomas Garrett, living in the state of Delaware, and a free black man, William Still of Philadelphia, and the alliance they formed as "friends of humanity" as they assisted runaways along the Eastern Line of the Underground Railroad. Grades 7–10.

Bial, Raymond. 1995. *The Underground Railroad.* Boston: Houghton Mifflin.

Color photo-essay and narrative overview of the Underground Railroad with a chronology of the antislavery movement in America. Includes a further reading list. Grades 4–8.

Burns, Bree. 1992. *Harriet Tubman and the Fight Against Slavery.* New York: Chelsea House.

Biography of the best-known African American conductor. Describes her childhood as a slave, her escape to the North, and her work in the

Civil War. Good black-and-white photographs and artwork. Includes a reading list, chronology, glossary, and index. Grades 4–8.

Carlson, Judy. 1989. *Harriet Tubman: Call to Freedom.* New York: Fawcett Columbine.

Biography of the runaway slave who returned to the South nineteen times to help others escape. A few black-and-white illustrations and photographs. Lists "other books you might enjoy reading." Grades 4–8.

Claffin, Edward B. 1987. *Sojourner Truth and the Struggle for Freedom.* New York: Barron's Educational Series.

Biography of the woman who was born a slave and dedicated her life to improving the living conditions of blacks following the Civil War. Illustrated with line drawings. Includes glossary, topics for discussion, map activity, reference book list, and index. Grades 4–8.

Collins, James L. 1991. *John Brown and the Fight Against Slavery.* Brookfield, CT: Millbrook.

The story of one of the most daring and controversial men in the history of civil rights. Discusses abolitionism, "Bleeding Kansas," the Pottawatomie Massacre, Harper's Ferry, and the trial and execution of Brown. Good treatment of difficult material. Grades 4–8.

Connell, Kate. 1993. *Tales from the Underground Railroad.* Austin, TX: Taintree Steck-Vaughn.

The history of the Underground Railroad related as a series of true stories about people who escaped or helped others escape. Would make a good chapter-a-day read-aloud book. Grades 4–8.

Cooper, Michael L. 1994. *From Slave to Civil War Hero: The Life and Times of Robert Smalls.* New York: Lodestar.

The story of Robert Smalls, the first slave to become a widely known Civil War hero when he liberated himself, three companions, and the cotton steamer Planter from Confederate hands. Smalls went on to fight for the Union cause and was eventually elected to the United States Congress. Fascinating, little-known story includes photographs and artwork of the period. Grades 4–8.

Dowers, Jeffrey S. 1992. *Levi Coffin: A Friend to the Slaves.* Richmond, IN: Friends United.

A quick, easy illustrated storybook that introduces students to the life and antislavery activities of the stationmaster known as the president of the Underground Railroad. Grades 4–6.

Goff, Margaret. 1980. *Freedom Crossing.* New York: Scholastic.

Fictional story of a girl who faces a moral dilemma when she learns that her father and brother are helping runaway slaves. She knows that assisting fugitives is breaking the law. But her concern for Martin Page, a twelve-year-old runaway, helps her resolve this conflict. Grades 4–8.

Gorrell, Gena K. 1996. *North Star to Freedom.* New York: Delacorte.

A comprehensive history of slavery, abolitionism, and the Underground Railroad, this book is well illustrated with photographs and artwork. Includes a chronology, source notes, suggested readings, and index. Grades 4–8.

Hurmence, Belinda. 1997. *Slavery Time When I Was Chillun.* New York: Putnam's Sons.

Narratives of life in slavery collected by the Federal Writers' Project in the 1930s. Generously illustrated with photographs. Includes a selected reading list on various aspects of slavery. Grades 4–8.

Levine, Ellen. 1988. *If You Traveled the Underground Railroad.* New York: Scholastic.

An overview of what the Underground Railroad was and how it worked. Illustrations on every page. Grades 4–8.

McKissack, Patricia. 1998. *Picture of Freedom: The Diary of Clotee, a Slave Girl.* New York: Scholastic.

A fictional story that takes place in 1859. Clotee, a slave girl, secretly teaches herself to read and write, something that is forbidden in the South. She eventually becomes a conductor on the Underground Railroad and must decide if she will plan her own escape. Grades 4–7.

Newman, Shilee P. 2000. *The African Slave Trade.* New York: Watts Library.

A history of slavery in Africa as well as in the United States with a particular emphasis on the living condition of slaves. Includes exceptional illustrations, a time line, a glossary, online sites, and an index. Grades 4–8.

Rappaport, Doreen. 1991. *Escape from Slavery: Five Journeys to Freedom.* New York: Harper Collins.

An accessible, well-organized book that gives a picture of the heroism of people escaping from slavery and those who helped them. Grades 4–8.

Smucker, Barbara. 1977. *Runaway to Freedom: A Story of the Underground Railroad.* New York: Harper Collins.

Fictional account based on actual slave narratives of two girls who escaped from a Mississippi plantation to Canada. Grades 4–8.

Educational Videos

Amistad, starring Morgan Freeman, Anthony Hopkins, Djimon Hounsou, and Matthew McConaughey. Produced by Steven Spielberg for Dream-Works Pictures in association with HBO. (Color, 2 hours, 35 minutes, VHS Motion Picture, R rating, 1998)

Based on a true story, this Academy Award–winning motion picture chronicles the incredible journey of a group of enslaved Africans who overtake their captors' ship, *La Amistad*, and attempt to return to their homeland. When the ship is seized, the captives are brought to the United States, where they are charged with murder and await their fate in prison. John Quincy Adams (played by Anthony Hopkins) successfully defends the Africans, who are free to return to their native land. Best for teachers to use this film for their own background.

Beloved, starring Oprah Winfrey, Danny Glover, Thandie Newton, Kimberly Elise, and Beah Richards. Produced by Ronald Bozman, Jonathan Demme, and Oprah Winfrey. (Color, 2 hours, 12 minutes, VHS Motion Picture, R rating, 1998)

Based on the Pulitzer Prize–winning novel by Tony Morrison, the film takes place near the end of the antebellum period. Sethe, a former slave played by Oprah Winfrey, is adjusting to a new life in freedom. But she is determined to prevent her own four children from experiencing the trauma of slavery and plans to kill them. Documents the evils of slavery as well as the meaning of family. Best for teachers to use this film for their own background.

The Freedom Station, starring Jada Pinkett. Written and produced by Scott Davies and Cheryl Magill. Maryland ITV. (Color, 28 minutes, VHS Drama, 1988)

Dramatization of the story of a runaway girl sheltered by a white family. Students may recognize a young Jada Pinkett in the lead role. Sweet story, good production values, and solid performances. Good springboard for a class discussion. Grades 6–12.

Lucretia Mott, starring Pamela Sommerfield. Produced by EPH Productions, P.O. Box 1042 Ansonia Station, New York, New York 10023. (Color, 60 minutes, VHS Drama, 1985)

Describes the reform activities of Lucretia Mott (1793–1880), a Philadelphia Quaker who was steadfast in her championing of abolitionism, women's rights, and peace. Filmed at historic sites in Philadelphia and Gettysburg, Pennsylvania.

Underground Railroad, hosted by Alfre Woodard. Produced by Triage for the History Channel. (Color, 100 minutes, VHS Documentary, 1998). ISBN 0-7670-1679-3

A thrilling story of a two-hundred-year-old struggle to break the bonds of slavery in the American South. Contains dramatic re-creations of escapes and acts of selfless heroism. Chronicles the achievements of such abolitionist figures as Frederick Douglass, Harriet Beecher Stowe, Harriet Tubman, and William Lloyd Garrison.

Whispers of Angels: A Story of the Underground Railroad, starring Ed Asner and Blair Underwood. Produced by Teleduction, 305 A Street, Wilmington, Delaware 19801. (Color, 60 minutes, VHS Docudrama, 2001)

A riveting docudrama based on the Underground Railroad activities of Thomas Garrett (played by Ed Asner) and William Still (Blair Underwood). With the help of the legendary Harriet Tubman, these two stationmasters assisted runaways from Maryland's Eastern Shore through the border state of Delaware to the free state of Pennsylvania. Interviews with scholars are integrated with dramatic narrative scenes, underscored with specially recorded period music.

Websites

African American Genealogy Group *www.aagg.org*

The African American Genealogy Group, based in Philadelphia, operates this site, which includes census records, birth, marriage, and death records, and historical newspaper archives in several states.

Kentucky's Underground Railroad *www.ket.org/underground/*

Highlights Kentucky's participation in the Underground Railroad and features oral history, teacher resources, and discussion forum.

Levi Coffin House *www.waynet.org/nonprofit/coffin.htm*

> The Levi Coffin House in Fountain City, Indiana, now a state historical site, was a major stop on the Western Line of the Underground Railroad. Site features photographs of the house museum and its original owners and a substantial list of links.

National Geographic's Underground Railroad *www.nationalgeographic.com/features/99/railroad*

> Complex and sophisticated website with excellent graphics, audio, educational resources, and links.

National Underground Railroad Freedom Center *www.undergroundrailroad.org/*

> Site features information on the Cincinnati-based museum, its Freedom Station program, and slavery's past; educational resources; lists of documented Underground Railroad agents and sites by state and county; opportunities to get involved in Underground Railroad research; and an e-newsletter.

National Underground Railroad Network to Freedom *www.cr.nps.gov/ugrr*

> This National Park Service website includes a history of the Underground Railroad, narratives of Underground Railroad activity, technical assistance to sites on the Network to Freedom, and a forum for discussion.

Slave Trade Data Collection *www.rootsweb.com/~afamerpl/slavetrade.html*

> This new and rapidly growing site has a rare collection of slave data. Organized around slave markets where slave auctions took place and Southern plantations.

The Underground Railroad Project *www.state.vt.us/vhs/educate/ugrr.htm*

> Funded by the Vermont Council on the Humanities, this site emphasizes slaves' escape to Canada through Vermont. Includes teaching packet and sections on the Colonization Society, Antislavery Society, and national and Vermont time lines.

Still Connected *www.undergroundrr.com/*

> Operated by the William Still Underground Railroad Foundation, this site contains abolitionist biographies, genealogy links, histories of the Underground Railroad and the Still family, and information about the annual Still Family Reunion Festival.

APPENDIX A: DOCUMENT ANALYSIS WORKSHEET

STUDENT NAME: _____

1. *What* kind of document is this? *What* is the document about?

2. *Who* wrote the document?
   Age: Sex: Occupation: Married/Unmarried:
   Children: Residence: Able to Write: Other Information:

3. *When* was the document written?

4. *Where* was the document written?

5. *Why* was the document written? For whom was it written? Does it reveal any bias?

6. *So, what* is the significance of the document? What conclusions can you draw?

APPENDIX B: PHOTO ANALYSIS WORKSHEET

Directions: Complete this chart and attach a photocopy of the photograph you have studied.

STUDENT NAME: _____

1. *First reactions:* Jot down whatever first impressions you get about the photograph itself, and the persons or objects in the photo. Describe your feelings.

2. *Detailed examination:* List all the observable facts in the photo.

   People   *Objects*   *Interior*   *Exterior*

3. *Facts known from other sources:* Indicate here the actual place and date of the photo if not on the photo itself, the names of the people portrayed, and so on.

4. *Characteristic expression or special relationships of persons or objects in the photograph:* Is the subject staring into the camera lens or away from it? Is there any noticeable expression? If so, how do you characterize it?

5. *Describe the mood of the photograph:* Formal, candid, happy, unhappy, indifferent. Explain your response.

6. *Considered reactions:* Jot down how you feel about the photograph now that you've studied it carefully and answered any questions you may have had.

©2005 by William C. Kashatus from *In Pursuit of Freedom*. Portsmouth, NH: Heinemann.